MISSING PAGES

A Novel by

Baland Iqbal

Missing Pages by Baland Iqbal
Published in 2022 by Meraj Publishing House, Canada
Translated by Anjum Baba
Cover design & formatting by Nabin Karna
Edited by Ken Darrow & Jozair Bland

Dedicated to those who live beyond race,
religion, color or nationality.

'It is just that within our power lies quill and tablet,
But what of our power to write the heart's truths?'
Himayat Ali Shair

CONTENTS

CHAPTER 1

The moment I looked into the eyes of that frail white woman, the silence and isolation of the room seemed to channel themselves into her silent eyes. Her eyes were as void as a bottomless abyss. There was simply nothing left in that lonely pair of eyes. Her aging eyes were devoid of any hope or longing, desire or wish; neither was there any love or indifference left. Those eyes were so devoid of color that they were not even fit to be called colorless. The bleakness in them had extinguished both light and darkness. Those eyes, without any trace of feelings or emotions, carried just a moment, a moment caught in the wheel of time, a thing of the past. And carrying this particular moment of a day long lost, she continued to exist.

Before I could untangle myself from the labyrinth of such intense thoughts her voice reached my ears and pulled me out of my trance. "Listen, would you like to drink something?"

My palpitating heart surfaced from the isolated ocean of her eyes and blabbered something of its own. "Yes, of course, tea would be fine."

I felt the thick air of the room was unable to bear my casual tone. Suddenly, the whole atmosphere appeared very light. This light environment resembled the moment when tiny cracks are formed before the shattering of glass. The way skin feels slight chills before the arrival of a cold breeze or eyes moisten before welling up with tears.

"I will get it," she said, rising from her nineteenth-century Victorian couch, but before she could rise completely, I stretched out my hands and stopped her.

"Please leave it, don't bother." Looking at my wrist, I said, "Guess I should be leaving now, else I will be late."

The old woman stared at me and uttered very softly, "I would have felt better had you stayed a little longer."

I exhaled a cold sigh. Removing my eyes from my wrist I looked at her; there was a faint flicker of pale colors in her eyes and her lips trembled to say something, but before she could start her sentence all the light began to diminish.

"I know you people from India and Pakistan are ever so formal in expressing your wishes. 'He' too was no different."

The same old isolation began to seep back into her eyes once again.

"Sit, I will get tea for you. I too want a cup at the moment." She rose from her chair and went towards the other end of the room slowly. There on the shelf, an electric kettle, teabags, sugar, milk, and teacups were placed in perfect order.

I shouldn't move, I thought and coalesced with the lush couch. The sofa exuded a damp smell indicating its dilapidated state; however, the fragrance of freshly starched covers succeeded in expelling that odor to a great extent. When I raised my eyes, I couldn't help taking

2

into view my whole surroundings—furniture, wallpaper, curtains hanging against the windows, and the carpet under my feet. The sturdy furniture made from the Indian rosewood had paled over the years, just like her. Purple-colored bright curtains, standing still against the window, had lost all their color and now they looked as bland and colorless as the murky carpet underneath. The crystal vase on the table was dried up of all water and its salt had severely affected its sheen. The lifeless plant had nothing but was hanging on to a few dead petals on top.

The sound of boiling water broke my trance and the steam evaporating from the kettle blurred whatever faint color the room housed. Once again, my eyes, against their accord, moved towards the corner and fixed on the old woman brewing tea for me. Placing the teabags into two cups, she poured boiling water from the kettle. The warm aroma of the tea brought back the feeling of life into the cold room. Placing the sugar and milk on the tray along with the two cups, she walked slowly towards me carrying the tea. I hurried from my place and went to her; taking the tray from her, I said very softly, "Please, give it to me, I will carry it."

"Alright." Walking towards the sofa she mumbled, "I know what you are thinking."

Taking the cup from her, I sat on the sofa and looked at her again.

"The place where we stay long enough, we are bound to become a part of it. Its belongings start to look like us and in turn we also start to look like our belongings. While I was brewing tea, you were talking to my belongings because I am existent in this furniture, the windows, doors, curtains, and this carpet."

I felt I had been caught red-handed. Taking a small sip, I said, "The tea is very good."

"So, you are here to take the pictures?" the old woman asked, ignoring my compliment altogether.

"Yes. I believe, with the help of those pictures, I can connect the pieces of lost history," I said, looking at her while placing my cup on the table.

"Is it really necessary?" she said after a pause, stressing each word.

"*Maybe?*" I instantly gulped down my mouthful of tea and replaced it with "Certainly."

 "And what would you gain out of all this?" Her voice still held the same strength.

"*Satisfaction.*" There, I once again faltered. Shutting my eyes tightly, I said, "Completion."

"But this is an extremely lengthy and confusing journey. Will you be able to hold on?" There was curiosity in her eyes.

"Yes." I sounded confident now.

Stretching out her hands, she picked up a gray-colored diary from the table. The diary appeared swollen by the loose pages and pictures stuffed in between its pages. With shivering hands, she opened it at the exact location where black-and-white photographs were placed. Pulling out the pictures from the diary, she kept it back in its place and stared at the pictures with blank eyes. She gazed at the pictures one after the other until she reached the final one, and then she handed me a few pictures. These photographs were more than fifty or sixty years old and had discolored so much that, instead of black and white, they looked more of a sepia tone. They appeared both aged and damp. It was quite evident that both years and tears had worn them out.

"I will return these pictures very soon, I promise." I stuffed the pictures inside my handbag, but then I suddenly realized there was suffering hidden behind her silence. Extending my hands, I held both of her trembling hands gently.

"These are your trust in my custody; I know how important they are to you."

"No, maybe you have no idea at all," she grumbled.

I could not fully understand the underlying meaning of her sentence. Silently, I looked at her eyes; her gaze was fixed on the floor.

"Okay, I will take my leave now else I will be actually late." I hurried out of the room and into the porch and straight out of the house. I felt I could no longer endure the silence and isolation of the old woman and her house; the isolation that stood on the dark abyss of never-ending pain and suffering.

The moment she shut the door, I felt a slight cry was also stifled by the sound of the closing doors. This gave rise to a silence behind me that got lost in the loud noise of the moving truck that passed by.

The bright light of the evening coined with long black hair doubled the depression. The chill lost between the final days of September and October was trying to find its place. Who knows whether it was destined for the cold long lonely nights or it was to face the lost memories of noon in the near future? The words of the old woman clung to my soul like a creeper around the branches of an olive tree.... I felt the uneasiness within me trying to get hold of the calmness outside.

Even the distance from the door to my car was restricted to just a few steps but it seemed to have got stretched over an entire century. My legs felt both light and heavy at the same time and I took one step and missed the next in a hurry. I opened the driver's seat, turned on the engine, gave a long lingering look at the old woman's house, and put all my weight on the accelerator.

Initially, I felt the house of the old woman float on the clouds instead of being tied to the ground, but in no time I shifted my attention towards the rows and rows of vehicles that sped away.

CHAPTER 2

In no time, all hell broke loose.

The dark clouds filled with water clashed and collided together creating explosive sounds. A kind of flood descended upon the earth from the sky in the form of innumerable tributaries. My heart felt benumbed by the constant explosion in the sky and my eyes were blinded by sporadic lightning. The wind cried and lamented in a fearful voice, it so felt as if it was mourning the cracking of the sky. There was chaos all around me. Sounds of climatic cries paired with my own sobs created great pandemonium. I was shivering and shaking with intense fear, it was certain that the sky would fall upon me at any moment. With trembling feet I tried to press the accelerator but my car appeared to have left the storm-leaden grounds and was floating in the air. It tossed and turned vehemently pulling me off my seat again and again. I was swaying left and right, and then suddenly I got a severe jolt that made me bolt from the vehicle and land outside. Without thinking anything, I rose and started to run frantically, covering my head and ears. I was running for my life.

There was smoke all around me. There was fire everywhere and then, suddenly, sinking deep inside the fat belly of the sky, smoke rose from all directions. It was difficult to breathe normally. Raising my head, I tried to gulp in smoky air and breathe normally and when there was no oxygen I gripped my neck with both hands and tried to breathe deeply looking up at the sky. Suddenly, I felt the entire sky had cracked open and was about to fall on me and I was sinking inside the earth unable to budge an inch from my location; my body sank deeper and deeper inside the ground.

My eyes snapped open. My hands held my neck as I sobbed bitterly. When I realized how tightly I had gripped my neck, my hands slackened and I took a deep breath, but this resulted in a convoluting fit of bone-shattering coughs.

Slowly and steadily, I regained composure and realized I was drenched in sweat and my clothes, which clung to my body, had turned frighteningly cold. Anxiously, my hands held my head, which was slowly becoming numb. For a while, I stayed on the bed breathing heavily, and then things became a little normal. It was then that I realized that all this was just a nightmare—a nightmare that benumbed me mentally and physically. After some time, when I was totally calm, I turned on the night lamp and sat on the edge of the bed staring at the wall and windows blankly. The alarm clock on the side table indicated the time, 03:25. The ticking clock screamed the silence of the room with every tick.

Gosh! What a terrifying nightmare, my body shuddered with fear.

Was it a dream or prophecy of some impending threat? My sinking heart gave rise to doubt.

I yawned. A small voice stirred within me unconsciously and escaped my lips without fear or stress.

For a moment, I tried to close my eyes once more, but then suddenly they snapped open.

8

I sat on the bed bolt upright, looked around and stared at the ceiling. The ceiling was wrapped in light and the shadow of the fan was thrown by the lamp in the room. A tall shadow of my figure hovered against the wall and moved every time I stirred. I thought to turn on the fan so that the room would feel less dense but dropped the idea looking at my sweat-soaked garment. The stickiness of my clothes replaced my fear with unease. I looked down and touched my clinging top and turned towards the wardrobe and rose to change into something dry and fresh. I had taken two steps towards the wardrobe but then suddenly, unknowingly, I went towards the window and moved the curtain slightly and glimpsed the porch below. The alley in front was covered in darkness and utter silence that was broken only by barking dogs. The sky was clear except for a few pieces of cloud playing hide and seek with the moon. I put back the curtain and walked towards the wardrobe.

After a while, when I entered the room wearing fresh clothes from the storeroom, I felt much better than before. Standing in front of the dressing table, I looked at my reflection in the mirror; it was quite evident my face had turned pale after waking up from a nightmare. My hair was lying messily on my shoulders, I held it with both hands and tied it in a bun, but as usual two ringlets escaped the bun and lay carelessly over my forehead and cheekbones. Out of habit, I pulled back the ringlet from my forehead and tried to tuck it behind my ears, but the stubborn hair again escaped the barricade of my ears and danced on my forehead. From the jug placed on a table in front of me I poured some water into a glass and took a big gulp, took a deep breath, and slumped in the bed.

What was all this? What kind of dream was that? Everything looked so vivid and real.

I shook my head slightly and tried to pull myself out of the trauma and then, lying sideways on the bed, I closed my eyes. I tried to relate yesterday's events with my own life one after another. Somehow, I was confident that yesterday's weird events were closely connected to the nightmare. One after another, various incidents danced in front of my eyes without any sync or order … and then, soon enough, there appeared a linear order to my cabal thoughts and I began to recall something.

Yesterday, the sky was cloudy in the morning only. It rained incessantly. No sooner had one cloud done crying than another one joined hands tearfully. After taking the photographs from the old white lady, I thought I would straightaway go home instead of driving elsewhere. I don't know what made me change my mind and I turned my car from Shahrah Faisal towards the National Stadium. Driving from Dalmia, the moment I looked at the road opposite the National Stadium I turned towards Gora Cemetery (a Christian graveyard). The graveyard was draped in depression after getting washed over by rain as if the rainwater had doubled its grief. It was not possible to take the car further inside the cemetery, which is why I parked it aside. And then, sitting silently inside my vehicle, I stared at the solitary space and let the isolation seep inside me deeply.

I remembered why I decided to be there suddenly. The old lady had told me that her son, in the prime of his youth, was laid to rest somewhere in this graveyard. This made my heart skip a beat; my mother too was resting there. However, it was a different matter; for a long, long time, I did not go there after her death mainly because this place filled me with immense sadness. I avoided it intentionally. I have no clue why, despite being a Muslim, my mother, in her will, insisted on being buried in a Christian graveyard.

I sighed. What a wet day it was yesterday. I thought of that old woman and the cemetery. The memories of my mother and the unnerving silence and depression of the graveyard put a wet blanket on my spirit. Reclining my driving seat a little at the back, I relaxed a little bit and closed my eyes. Suddenly, loud thunder reverberated around the whole place and torrential rain engulfed my closed space. I woke up with a start and was benumbed by the sight of a man dressed in shabby rags, pulling at the handle of my car. He pulled the handle with one hand and with the other hand banged the window frantically as if he would break it if I didn't open it. My heart began to beat hard and my hands and legs shook with fear. I pulled the door with all my might and tried to lock it, but it gave way. Against my fierce struggle, he opened the entire door and tried to bend over me; to save myself from him, I tried to push both his hands away from my body. Initially, I thought he was there to attack me, but he pulled my pendant forcefully and then moved toward the photographs lying on the passenger's seat.

I mustered all my strength and tried to throw him out. I was lucky he slipped and fell back to the ground. He hurled profanities at me. Following my sheer instinct, I locked the door and with shaky hands I tried to start the car. I tried to change gears one after another, and the moment I saw the car was in reverse gear, I pushed the accelerator forcefully. The car jerked to attention like an airplane and with screeching tires rushed back at full speed. With a loud noise, my car hit the main gate of the graveyard. The man ran after me, but the rain and mud were making it difficult for him to run faster. For a moment, I tried to catch the trunk of the car, but his hands slipped and he fell flat on the ground. I put the car in first gear, pressed the accelerator with total strength, and fled out of the graveyard. Everything happened so fast; I didn't even know when exactly I left Dalmiya Road and reached the National Stadium.

I continued to drive in panic and once again reached Shahrah Faisal. By now, the rainwater covered the windscreen in tiny rivulets. My whole body was shaking with fear. I parked my car and composed myself, and instead of turning towards mine, I headed to Atya's home.

By the time I neared Atya's house, my heartbeat had normalized a little, but my condition was still not very stable. My whole body trembled uncontrollably as if there was something planted beneath my shoulder and, beyond my will, it made me shiver and shake all over. Even though the cold sweats on my forehead had dried, my entire body was sweating profusely and my clothes clung to my skin. I was both intimidated and panicked simultaneously. I was afraid, thinking that man was hiding somewhere inside my car. The filth and stain clinging to my body as a result of the scuffle made me feel filthy and tainted both inside and out.

Not even in my wildest dreams could I have imagined that I would face such an ordeal in the melancholy environment of the graveyard that would turn my depression into a state of pure frenzied chaos. By the time I reached Atya's house, I had literally turned around innumerable times to check the back seat and the windshield to make sure that man was not inside the car with me.

Atya is my friend from my university days. While I was doing my master's in journalism, she was enrolled in the history department. Before she could complete her master's degree, she got married to a doctor. It has been two years now, but am still not over Asad, my first love whom I met during my M.A. Atya was pleasantly surprised to see me at her door initially, but the moment she looked at my disheveled condition her smile was replaced by clear signs of worry.

She blurted, "Are you alright, Fatma? Whatever happened to you?"

Holding my hand, she pulled me inside her home and locked the main door. I shrugged off her hand and then instantly grabbed it once again trying hard to get a grip of my senses. Atya took me inside the living room and I collapsed on the sofa. I was yet to utter a single word and there were clear signs of worry etched all across Atya's face. After a while, she handed me a glass of water given to her by the house help. She might have indicated to him to do so with her eyes. Taking a sip, I exhaled deeply and narrated the entire tale to her. I could see with each word that escaped my mouth and was strung into a sentence the concern and worry evaporated from her face slowly.

Finally, when I had finished, she said, "Fatma, it was just an accident and you brought it on yourself.

"You are well aware of the situation in the city, it's worse than a jungle. If a young girl is found alone in a graveyard, a druggie beggar is bound to pounce and consume her. You know the situation better than I do, don't you? Well, you are a journalist, who else would be more aware of the city's condition? Dude, come on now, show me the pictures of that old woman's son. You feel that the man attacked you because of the photographs; it is just your assumption. In reality, he wanted to snatch your purse, which was lying next to the photographs.

"By the way, how old was he?" Atya asked.

"Around fifty to sixty, I guess, or maybe he was young. Well, how would one know the age of these drug addicts?" I replied.

I took out the photographs given to me by the old woman and handed them to her. It was a four-or-five-decades-old photograph of a white kid standing next to a young woman, most probably his mother. Atya flipped over the photograph, at the back something was written in a foreign language. Atya switched on the laptop and logged into Google Translate to check what exactly was written. Those incomprehensible scripts were the names of two people— Zosia Casnova and Peter Casnova.

My eyes lit up on seeing this.

"My guess was right." I looked at Atya with meaningful eyes.

"What do you mean?" She looked into my eyes.

"I'll tell you but I need to confirm something with that old lady, what's her name, yes, Zosia Casnova," I muttered, thinking of something else.

"I don't understand a thing," Atya said, rubbing her temple as she looked at the picture.

"Wait." I took out a small black envelope from my purse and handed it to her. "Look at this."

"What is this?" Atya took the envelope from my hand and looked inside. There were a few pages where something was written im black and red ink and a few black-and-white photographs. Before I could say anything, Atya's servant entered the living room once again and said, "Ma'am, I have served the food."

Atya told me, "Come on now, go to the washroom and freshen up. First we will eat and then we'll talk about it."

Saying this Atya went towards the kitchen and I headed to the washroom. After dinner, we returned to the living room. Atya picked up the envelope from the table and pulled out a picture from it.

"Dude, isn't it the picture of the same kid you showed me just now? Is it from the same European lady, what's her name Zosia, yes Zosa Casnova?" Atya pronounced her name with great difficulty.

"No, Atya. The day before yesterday, I found these pictures and pages in a black envelope inside Ammi's diary. Look, here too in the Polish language it is written Zosia Casnova and Peter Casnova," I told her suspiciously.

Atya held the pages and mumbled, "Bro, I have a hunch that whoever has written these knows a couple of foreign languages. Look, there is English, and then there is Polish, and look at this, it looks like Bengali or Hindi … isn't it? Hey, your mother was also from Bengal, right?"

"Yes, Ammi was from Bengal, which is why she knew a little bit of Bengali too. It is not Hindi, it is Bengali written in certain places on these pages."

Atya stared at the pages, she then looked at me and thought about something after which she gave a slight shrug and became silent.

When I saw her shrugging her shoulder, I asked, "What do you mean?"

"No, nothing." She was clearly nervous. "Nothing, nothing at all."

"No, no, say it out loud or else I will do so," I said, looking straight into her eyes.

"Don't you wanna say that I look less a Paki and more a cross breed mix of Bengali and European genes?" I stated without looking away.

"Yes, maybe you are right, Fatma," Atya replied.

"Never mind, I don't know what's true and what's not...." This time it was I who shrugged.

"Alrighty then, I gotta leave now. I am very tired; in fact, it was a really long day today."

I sighed then yawned. "I want a long peaceful sleep once I'm home. I need to go to the office tomorrow, plus I have accumulated too many backlogs," I said, rising from the sofa.

"Listen." Atya called her servant. "Shall I send Shams with you? He will drive right behind and drop you home safely."

"Come on. I don't have goons chasing me. No need to worry. It was just an accident. These things are quite common in this city. Gotta go now, see you."

I collected the photographs and papers, put them inside my bag, took my keys, and left.

After starting the car, I looked in the rearview mirror, Atya remained rooted to her door till the time my car left her alley and entered Shahrah Faisal Road.

On reaching home, I took a long hot bath. After which I collapsed on my bed. In no time I crashed and was lost in a deep sleep followed by that terrifying nightmare.

CHAPTER 3

The next morning, when I woke, my eyes fell on the wall clock as usual. It was seven in the morning. I breathed a sigh of relief and thought, *Thank God I still have an hour left until I need to be at work.* The moment I closed my eyes I began to miss Asad. The moment he got posted to Kashmir, we stopped communicating over the phone. He had made it very clear that for a while both of us would have to stay connected via email alone. He assumed that in the army everybody's phone was tapped and there was no scope for personal affairs in that arena. Asad had joined ISI a year and half back. During that time, he had been extremely busy. From the moment India abrogated article 370 and 35A, ISI had been agile in the Gilgit Baltistan and Azad Kashmir regions.

Will the soft, poetic heart of Asad get subjugated by the harsh minds of the army personnel? I thought.

I will email him after returning from the office, I have loads to tell him, I decided.

On my way to the office, when the car stopped at the red light of Teen Hatti Bridge, suddenly begging women and a couple of slum children surrounded my car. For a second, I saw the same hopelessness in their eyes that was evident in the eyes of that old woman. I saw there was a long stretch of slum dwellings underneath the bridge. Smoke rose from the earthen stoves, women tried to light it by fanning it with a broken tattered hand fan or blowing on it through cylindrical pipes. The naked kids sitting around the women either slapped away the flies hovering around them or wailed loudly out of hunger. Taking out a few coins from my purse, I handed them over to the beggars at the signal and tried to speed away; at that very moment, a boy stretched out a newspaper in my direction and said, "Ma'am, hot news! India has turned Kashmir into Palestine!"

"Gosh! Same depressing news." I pulled up the window. That day, the traffic was heavier than usual. Either there was a political congregation in the city or maybe an army parade; whatever the cause, there was a weird rush. The trauma of yesterday's incident at the graveyard and the nightmare was still fresh. It took me a total of 45 minutes to reach Metropol Hotel. My office was located just opposite it on the second floor. I parked the car and, instead of taking the elevator, I came out of the back gate of the hotel and moved towards the gallery. Suddenly, I felt someone standing in the gallery staring at me. Initially, I thought he must be some random guy. As it is, in this city it is quite common to eye the girls, but from his appearance, he did not look like some random guy. He was a well-dressed man in his 60s. It was evident from his suave personality and overbearing demeanor that he was a CEO or an industrialist. The way he looked at me said something else; it seemed as if he recognized me and was trying to decide where he'd seen me before.

Maybe someone told him about me secretly and now he is here to meet me, I thought.

But the female ego within me refrained me from initiating the conversation, and ignoring him completely I went past him even without giving him a second glance. Before I could take a step toward the stairs, I heard his voice.

"Excuse me, can I talk to you?"

Even though I had seen it coming, I still feigned surprise and, putting extra stress into my voice said, "Sorry," and stood still. I was right; from his gray sideburns it was obvious he must have been in his 60s. He had deep intelligent eyes and a broad forehead that bespoke wisdom.

"Yes please?" I asked him in a very calm tone.

"My name is Tahseen Jafri and I am into publication. You may have heard of Famous Books Publications. I am one of the managers of that firm. If am not wrong you are Fatma Hasan, right?" He addressed me very gently.

"Yes, please tell me what it is. I am Fatma," I said.

Owing to my journalism background, I was aware that various magazines of this city were printed by this publishing house and undoubtedly Famous Publications was one of the renowned publications of Pakistan.

"Well, the only thing is that in my neighborhood, at Phase Six, lives an old lady named Sophie. Today, early morning, she knocked on my door and handed over your visiting card to me. She has asked me to talk to you. She wants her photographs back. She was restless throughout last night and didn't get to sleep a bit. She was telling me that I should take those photographs from you today and hand them over to her in the evening lest she falls ill. Initially, I thought I must give you a call, but when I saw your card, I realized your office is right next to mine. My office is right here in Awari Tower.

I thought of meeting you before going to the office in case I forgot about it."

"Aha." I put my hands inside my bag but then something crossed my mind and I moved from the stairs and stood in the gallery. "Wait a minute," I told him. I dialed Zosia Casnova's number on my mobile phone and within a short while someone from the other end said, "Hello."

"Yes, it's Fatma calling. I have your neighbor Tahseen Jaffri with me. Do you want your photographs back?"

I told her the photographs were at my house and was in the office now. Would it possible for me to deliver the photographs tomorrow at her place by myself? I would like to spend more time with her. After speaking with Zosya, I thanked Mr. Jafri and informed him that I had spoken with her and that I was going to drop the photographs off to her personally.

After Tahseen Jaffri's departure, I returned to the stairs and headed towards my office.

Post office, the same old rush hour and heavy traffic awaited me. The whole city had congregated together at Mazar e Quaid to protest against the Kashmir issue. The protest march flowed around the region like anxious tributaries. On one side there were people from trade unions, whereas in other places there were lawyers; in some areas, there were political activists while in some places students were raising their voices. In every other car, people were seen wearing bandanas carrying the message "Kashmir Will Become Pakistan" or raising a banner saying the same. After every pause and break the cry of Allah o Akbar was heard. This time, 40 minutes' journey to home was covered in two hours. The service road became of help and somehow I managed to pull the cab out of the narrow lane and covered the area from Metropol to Nursery in one hour and 40 minutes. I reached home at 7:30 in the evening. Right after dinner, I crashed. I woke up at around 11 and sat with my laptop and a cup of tea by my side. My mood was a little heavy and all I wanted was to be near Asad. I wanted him to listen to my heartbeat, wished to tell him everything I told myself only. If only I could pour out all my feelings to him in words. There was pin drop silence in the room that was broken by the constant tap tap tap sound of my fingertips hitting the keyboard and piercing my open wounds.

I recalled a poem by Tagore.
I have not asked you anything
I have not told you my name
I stood silently
All alone by the well
The place where fell
The slanting shade of the tree
All my friends have left for their homes
The water pitcher is filled to the brim
Carrying it on the heads
Everyone called me and said
Come along with us
It's about to be noon
Never did I pay any attention
Stood right there
Lost in memories

When you arrived
I heard your nearing footsteps
When my eyes fell upon you
Your eyes were all dreary
In a very soft voice, you said that I

Am a thirsty traveler
Startled was I
From wide-eyed dreams
I poured the water from the pitcher
Onto the cup of your palm
The leaves above my head
Began to sway
And from some unknown source
The cuckoo began to sing
Right there the blossomed lilies
Gave out sweet fragrances
And merged in the air

When you had asked me my name
Then, shyness made me remain silent
And I stood there at my place
I did not say a thing
If ever my memories make you cry
To give you water
And to quench your thirst
This image clings to my heart
Even till now
Its sweetness will never be lost
The day is slowly coming to an end
And sorry am I
The song is nothing but a bird
And on my head
The neem leaves dance and sway
Here I am, sitting all alone
Thinking and thinking alone

Asad, you are well aware of the fact that your departure has turned
my life into a barren land, aren't you? I pine for your mere shade

night and day. All that I am left with are your fond memories, and I am all alone, lonely and isolated frantically running around on my quest. It is your loving words that are keeping me alive. Listen, Asad, I am getting tired now, I am in constant fear; I keep myself busy working relentlessly but my mind is not, for a second, free of your thoughts. Asad, I feel I am not going to meet that poet from my university again, one whose eyes were intoxicated by the wine of love and whose words carried the sweet fragrance of gentle emotion. One whose hands carried the paintbrush and his canvas had my sketches. One whose flowers are still pressed between the pages of my diary and their smell wafts through the diary like an exotic perfume. Does that guy remember whether I met him for real or was it just a dream? Which pleasant spring morning was it when the two of us became one? Which evening of fall was it that drove us apart?

Asad, yesterday I met a woman who has made friends with her solitude. One such woman who made me feel that her heart is filled with sand and only sand. For the first time, I saw a desert housed inside someone's body. For the first time I realized when solitude seeps inside one's soul then isolation becomes one's destiny. Yesterday, for the first time after meeting someone, I got intimidated and prayed to my Lord that never should loneliness be my punishment. That woman told me that for the last 40 or 50 years she has been regularly visiting the graveyard to meet her child but now she has decided that she will not go to the cemetery anymore. She said that last night she offered her final flowers to him and now she wants to forget this heart-wrenching fact that her bright young son is finally dead. What do you think? Is it really possible? Is she going to forget him? It is quite possible she is now tired of carrying the burden of her child. Maybe, what she thinks to be grief is not grief anymore but, just like her son, is ash and dust. I am scared, Asad, the love between you and me might turn into ash and dust soon. Is it really possible? Day and night I miss you in my heartbeat; I feel you in my breath and see you in my dreams; I feel you in me and my system at all times. Whenever I speak with you I get a feeling of completion. What am I to do, Asad?

My fingers continued to dance on the keyboards of my laptop and my heart quivered for Asad. And without my knowledge, I don't know when I left my world and entered the zone of Asad. I began to lose myself in his warm embrace and the touch of his strong lips against my soft ones brought me back to life. I could feel his deep kiss in every pore of my body. In no time, his hands moved towards my waist and pulled me closer to him and I got lost in his broad chest. And then a few of his careless locks on his forehead began to tease my half-open eyes. When I closed my eyes shyly, he began to kiss my face, caress my bosom and feel my nape like an obsessed lover. Finally, I surrendered myself to him.

He continued to make love to me and I fell deeper and deeper in love with him. There was a thirst within me that wasn't getting quenched and there was a thirst in him that continued to rise. There were no words, no thoughts between the two of us; except for love there was no other emotion between us. We are talking of love but no words were involved, we were expressing love without voice, and our bodies silently merged into each other. He continued to penetrate deep inside me and I continued to melt under him. In a moment of self-surrender, I began to collapse in his strong arms, and very slowly I was losing myself.

There was no track of time and don't know when the night came to an end. I woke up and grabbed the bedside clock; the time was 06:00. The light was on and the laptop with its lid open was lying there in the corner wherein my love mail before reaching Asad had already elevated my night with an enchanting dream. Lying down on the bed, a smile spread across my face and I looked at mine and Asad's photo on the desk. I took a deep sigh and then something crossed my mind that made me bite my lower lip and I shut my eyes tight.

CHAPTER 4

The next morning was Saturday. I was swooning and feeling intoxicated by the previous night's dream. My mind kept wandering in the wildness of Asad's romance, but then I drifted towards Zosia Casnova and then the incident of the graveyard and Atya's words engulfed me. I reached that lady after so much difficulty and acquired those photographs from her so that I could see if there was any difference between her photographs and the pictures lying in my mother's diary. It was an astonishing fact that both the pictures were of the same kid. What exactly was that European child's picture doing in my mother's diary? What was it that my mother was keeping from me? Why did she bring me from Dhaka to Karachi? Who was that man in the graveyard? Atya says he wanted my purse, but I remember it vividly; he looked at the photographs with a strange light in his eyes. His restlessness and mad desire to snatch the pictures from me with total force, he didn't even care about his life. All this felt so bizarre and everything was shrouded in great mystery as if there was some giant secret behind all this. One big secret that had strung all these events together.

When he pounced on me and went over me towards the back seat, I am sure his motive was to get those pictures. The pictures I brought from Zosia. I feel all the while I was lying with my eyes closed inside the cab he must have been glaring at the pictures from outside and was trying to recollect something. The way he jumped on those pictures, what exactly was that? And when he could not succeed, how badly did he try to stop the car? There was definitely something behind all this. I was lost in my thoughts when, suddenly, my mobile phone cried loudly and broke my chain of thoughts.

It was Zosia on the other side with her thick Polish accent.

"Fatma, I am waiting for you. You promised me."

I replied in the affirmative and confirmed that I would be there soon.

"Fatma, make sure you bring those pictures. I am used to going off to sleep looking at 'em. You see I couldn't sleep last night either," Zosia Casnova told me.

"Definitely, I will surely get those pictures to you today, but I have some other things to discuss with you as well." I got straight to the point without further ado.

"Why not, Fatma? You are a nice girl, I love talking to you," she said.

"It's nine o'clock right now," I said, looking at my watch. "I will try my best to reach you by ten."

"Alright, I will hang up now." Zosia cut the call.

What am I to do? I thought.

Two months back, when I was sorting my mother's stuff, I found a few pictures from her diary and some pages written in Bengali, English, and a European language, which she had kept very securely in a plastic pouch. From that day on, I was continuously looking for

Europeans residing in Karachi. There were quite a few families living in the posh locality of Defense Colony and Clifton. These past months I had met various families making several excuses and showed the picture from my mother's diary. Unfortunately, none of the families knew anything about that kid in the photo. Finally, I came to know about Zosia Casnova from one of my colleagues who stayed next to his house in Defense, Karachi. I met her through his reference and this time my excuse was that I was a social worker associated with an NGO and was surveying the Europeans living in Karachi. I asked her for the child's picture on the pretext that we needed black-and-white pictures of the European kids for our magazine. The excuse of black-and-white pictures for the colored magazine worked perfectly and that European lady handed me the photographs only on one condition—that I would keep them only for a day. It was such a pleasant surprise that the photograph in my mother's diary and Zosia Casnova was of the same child. My next target was to focus on Zosia and try to unearth the relationship between her and my family.

She opened the door after a single ring of the bell and took me to the same living room where I had sat with her last, the place where we had our first interaction. No sooner did I sit on the couch than I took out the envelope of photographs from my purse and placed them on the table in front of her. She readily picked up the envelope and took out the photographs from it. Zosia stared at the pictures silently. After some time, she went back to her bloated diary from where she had taken out the pictures last time. She put the photographs back in their old place.

It was time for me to set out on my quest; I asked her with great enthusiasm, "Can I ask you something?"

"Sure, why not?" she replied in a soft frail voice.

It was the first time I addressed her by her first name. "Ma'am, I know your name is Zosia and not Sofia. Zosia Casnova. Is it possible for me to address you as Zosia, please?"

"Absolutely positive, my dear. It felt great to hear my name after so long. I am glad you pronounced my name properly; most of the time, people mispronounce it and address me as Sofia. In fact, I have also got so used to being called Sofia that now I too feel that I am Sofia and not Zosia." She continued to talk in the same soft voice and then put forward a question. "By the way, how do you know my full name?"

"Actually, I saw yours and your son's name written at the back of your photograph and then looked up its exact pronunciation on Google multilingual dictionary. It is from there I came to know your real name and also your son's name, which is Peter." I told her everything very honestly.

"Oh!" This was all she could say in reply.

"Zosia, how long have you been in Pakistan?" I tried to move the discussion further.

"I was around nineteen or twenty years old when I first came to Pakistan from Germany. Everything looks like a century old now," Zosia replied, her gaze fixed at nowhere in particular.

"Why did you migrate from Europe to here or did you feel the cost of living would be less here or was it the beach that brought you here?" I stretched the discussion in the most subtle manner possible.

Zosia inhaled deeply and, without looking at my eyes, she said, "I so wish this had been the case! Those are very lucky who shift from one place to another place keeping the weather in mind. Lucky are those who get to select and settle in a place as per their mood. For us, survival was the only criterion. We just wanted to save ourselves from the so-called social animals or lose ourselves in the abyss of grief that lingered in our eyes. At that time, any place in the world that provided us a safe sanctuary was to be our next home; you can consider Karachi to be that safe sanctuary where I came to spend the rest of my life. But I will not complain; Karachi never let me feel neglected. The people here are very warm and welcoming. I never faced any trouble here."

"Where exactly did you live in Europe? Did you live in Germany alone or was it Poland? As you can see, I googled your name and came to know it's a polish name." I looked at her inquisitively.

"Oh dear! This is a really long tale." Zosia looked at me affectionately and it was the first time she addressed me so warmly.

"First tell me, do I prepare breakfast for you or will you be happy with tea alone?" she asked.

"You see I had breakfast only a while ago and took tea on my way to your place," I replied gratefully.

"Alright, no problem, but make sure you tell me straightaway without any formalities if you need anything. We aged people tend to feel youthful in the company of young people. Your arrival in my silent house fills it with youthful energy and positive vibes."

Her reply showed in her voice a combination of happiness and grief, and then she continued to speak in the same cheerful melancholic tone....

This is a story that belongs to the era of World War II. It was a time when the oppression of the Nazis made all the Jews settled across

Europe run for their lives. The infamous Holocaust is no secret to the young and the old. Everyone is well aware of the incident, but those that had to live through the horrors of the Nazi oppressions still get nightmares, even though half a century has passed since the terror. But as they say in the African proverb, the axe forgets but the tree remembers; same is the case with those who had to live through those horrifying times.

Our condition was just like the rest of the Jews; we were cornered on all sides and could not trust anyone. Poland was literally drenched in blood, the Jews were slaughtered mercilessly. All the lanes and by-lanes were filled with dead bodies. Not only Poland, but many also left Eastern Europe and entered Russia and from there they fled to Central Asia and South Asia, especially India, with the sole purpose of saving their lives.

Later on, this area of Karachi came to the side of Pakistan, and then two years later the UN declared Israel an independent state. At that time, around two to three thousand Jews from here moved to Israel. Initially, I too wanted to shift to Israel, but then, with a certain twist of events, I could not relocate and embraced this country as my own and belonged to it.

This was something totally new to me. I asked her, surprised, "Really? I had no idea there once lived so many Europeans in Karachi. So far I was under the impression that the majority of the residents here are Indian migrants that migrated here during the partition in 1947 or there are people here from other regions who come here in search of employment." Suddenly I was reminded of my own background and added to the ongoing discussion, "A few Bengalis who came here after the partition of 1971 in search of employment and a few Rohingyas refugee Muslims from Burma settled somewhere around here."

"No, not at all," Zosia said. "This is not the case, Fatma. Karachi houses people from all over the world. In fact, way before the partition of India, apart from Britishers, Russians, Americans, and Europeans too resided here. Then, slowly and gradually, each of them returned to their own nations. But even now, there are various pockets of Karachi even today where people of various ethnicities from Afghanistan, Kirgizstan, Iran, China, Philippines, and Sri Lanka reside."

I was listening to everything that Zosia said with rapt attention. I realized that never ever did I take any interest in the biostatics of my own city, which is why my knowledge of the people living here was so weak and ill-informed.

"Alright then, what happened after your people came here?" I once again tried to connect back to Zosia's life.

When Zosia saw the topic being steered back to her life once again, she gave a painful smile and said, "My life is a book of pain and languishment. Fatma, there is nothing other than calamities and tales of tribulations in my story."

"Still, I would want to listen to a bit but only as far as you deem fit. Don't you think when you share your grief it kind of decreases a little?" I tried to convince her in my own way.

"Yeah, it helps in catharsis but never ever eases the pain; in fact, at times, it only elevates. But I won't disappoint you, my dear girl. You are really very nice." She moved further away after consoling me. I felt she was talking more to herself than me.

Within a minute, I could hear Zosia's voice coming from the well and I found it feasible not to speak further.

"Look Fatma, some people are born to turn into fuel that is used in the ideological wars of other people. They don't have any say or stand in anything that goes on around them. All they ever want is a simple, uneventful life, a life where they have no hatred or rage for others; but, unfortunately, these innocent victims become a target of others' hatred and rage. I am also one of those innocent victims, to date I have not come to know the reason for being punished so viciously all my life. But one thing is for sure; I learned the lesson of countering hate with hate and this feeling of immense hatred cost me all my happiness and made me lose everything I held dear. Hate is a very bad thing, one should not even hate one's own self, but what was I to do back then? The fire within me didn't extinguish and turn me into ash. On the contrary, the fire of hatred only got ferocious with time. Alas! What can be done now? I don't have anything left in life. In fact, now the days of my life are quite limited and I don't have enough time to think of all the things that I lost. Now all I ever want is to live the rest of my life happily and in total harmony. I wish to be free of this pain, the pain of this life, as soon as possible."

Zosia stared at me for some time, and then, with shaky hands, she lifted the diary from the table and, looking at it, she said, "My girl, I am enclosed in this diary. It is my whole life but some pages are lost and I have no idea where they went. At times, I feel I never wrote those pages. This too is a fact that those were the most important pages that are not present in this diary, but I will read out those pages to you, the pages that were written with blood on the walls of my heart filled with bitter tears. I am afraid my words might wound you."

Zosia looked at me sadly and then silently she opened her diary. With her finger on the first page, she looked at me and started. "It happened in August 1943. World War II was on. I was around eight or nine years old at that time. We lived in Warsaw, the capital of Poland. There, in one of the Ghettos of Dola, we lived. Ghettos are actually the slum-like localities of the Jews."

And gradually, Zosia left me and got lost in the days of her past.

I remember that particular evening so vividly. Maybe Mama was unwell, which is why her face was so red and tensed. The droplets of sweat stayed on her sharp aquiline nose for some time, shivered a little, and then dropped, but the flow of the droplets was incessant. She continued to sweat profusely. I have no clue whether it was just her sweat or if it was mixed with her tears as well because her eyes were redder than her face. They were bloodshot. Her palms were burning hot as one of them held on to the back of my neck and I could feel the warmth burn my skin. It actually felt as if her burning hands were like hot tongs that would leave burn marks on my slender neck. Hurriedly, she fed me porridge from the other hand. It was actually a bowl full of breadcrumbs dipped in milk and my mother fed me with a spoon from it. Every time each morsel passed through my throat, I blinked heavily and in that particular moment I could see a veil fall over my eyes and my mama's scarf that was wrapped tightly around her forehead, and everything faded but then Mama's tear-streaked red face danced; her runny nose and bloodshot eyes danced in front of my eyes. I could see that my mother was trying to cover herself and benumb her headache with her scarf at the same time. In fact, the tightly wrapped scarf around my mother's head was in total contrast to my father's kippa, which hung loosely on his head. Still, it never came off whether he walked, stayed still, or lay on the bed.

Papa was lying silently on the couch nearby very silent and still. I have no clue whether he was still awake or asleep because many times, when he used to be too exhausted, he used to fall asleep as soon as he hit the sofa. But mostly, he gazed at the floor silently. Day in and day out occupation at the factory erased the difference between the color of his skin, clothes, and shoes. Every day, he returned from the factory drenched in his own suit wrapped in dirty rags for clothes. The factory had been closed for the past few days and this is why he was still home. Of course, the war had shut down everything; roads were filled with more uniformed soldiers and fewer civilians, every now and then the sound of explosives and gunshots reverberated through the region, the sound of bombs was disturbing my father's sleep and he was finding it hard to rest. He continuously tossed and turned on his couch. At times, he sat there holding his head and then once again would collapse on the couch and stare at the ceiling with blank eyes. More than worry, fear, and anxiety lurked in his eyes.

Mama raised her eyes and looked at Papa once, maybe she wanted to ask him something, but due to some internal turmoil she decided otherwise and pursed her lips, and in the meantime, she pushed another morsel into my mouth. Those morsels mixed with her anxiety slid down my throat and passed through my intestines. The food tasted bland and dusty, I was not enjoying my meal one bit. One of the reasons might be a lack of or little milk in the bread. Mama mainly fed me bread with cheese or dipped generously in goat milk, but on that particular occasion it felt as though there was literally nothing left in the house except for a few pieces of stale tough bread that were dipped in water and softened. Only a few spoonfuls of milk were added to the water and bread to change the taste, there was no sign of cheese or any other dairy products whatsoever. Not even a pound of fresh bread.

Mama and Papa had been starving for the last two days. I was lost in these disturbing thoughts when suddenly there was a banging sound at the door that broke the eerie silence of the room and created an environment of great terror. Papa suddenly sat bolt upright as if he had been hit by lightning and then at the same lightning speed he rose from the couch. Mama looked at the jangling door first and then at Papa with clear signs of horror evident in her eyes. Horrified, she hugged me with all her might. Papa looked at the door anxiously. His eyes were bulging with fear and anxiety. Initially, he looked at the door with his hands closed in a tight fist, but then he thought of something else and moved a little closer to the door and tried to look outside through the tiny crevices of the door.

Bang, bang, bang! This time, when the door shook violently, a shaky cry escaped his throat.

"Katwest?" (Who is it?)

"Yu yak Joseph." (Uncle Josef)

A soft stifled voice was heard from the other side of the door.

Papa breathed a sigh of relief and hurriedly unlatched the door. No sooner had he set the door ajar slightly than Uncle Josef, his wife Aunt Rebecca and their two sons Jacob and Aidan, who were two or four years older than me, rushed inside our house. As soon as they hustled inside, Papa locked the door once again. Uncle Josef and Aunt Rebecca looked exactly like Papa and Mama, scared and terrorized. I could see Jacob and Aidan also looked traumatized.

"Jacky, saip zof?" (Is everything alright?)

"Niye." (No) Uncle Josef said, sitting on the sofa.

"Zay wish." (Bad news) "Nazi zabih naas." (Nazis have started slaughtering the people openly)

Hearing this Papa held his head in his hands and slumped next to him on the sofa. Mama rose from her place and went to stand next to Aunt Rebecca. She began to sob, hugging her tight. As soon as I was released from Mama's grip, I ran towards Jacob and Aidan who were standing in the corner of the room silently. Terror and fear reigned supreme in the room.

Mama and Aunt Rebecca continued to sob like that while standing in the middle of the room; then Uncle Josef got up from the sofa and went towards them and whispered something in their ears. God knows what he said to them, Aunt Rebecca burst into bitter tears. She then went to the other room with Mama. Both Mama and Aunt Rebecca raised their hands and began to pray or rather beg tearfully. On the other side Papa and Uncle Josef were looking at me; Jacob and Aidan started to say something to each other. Maybe our parents were worried about us because they continued to look at us and clasped and unclasped their fingers. I was beyond myself with worry. I could feel my heart getting heavier with each passing minute.

I had finally realized the gravity of the situation.

Within a few minutes, there was a loud explosion. Before we could realize what struck us, all the windows and doors of our house came down in pieces. A lot of German soldiers entered our house screaming and shouting. They grabbed Uncle Josef and Papa by the hair and neck very roughly. They dragged them out of the house mercilessly. All this happened so fast that Papa and Uncle Josef didn't even get a moment to collect themselves and realize what exactly hit them. They could not even scream or protest and within a moment just Jacob Aidan and I remained still in the house.

Mama and Aunt Rebecca ran after them screaming and crying; at that moment, a German soldier punched my mother in her face and another one kicked Aunt Rebecca on her back. On their way out they banged the back of the gun so hard on our threshold that a big hole was formed in the middle of it. The three of us ran towards Aunt Rebecca and Mama and cried so hard hugging them so tightly. Nobody knew where they had taken Papa and Uncle Josef. It was a heartbreaking moment when I saw them for the last time; after that I have no clue what exactly happened to them. Did the sky suck them in or the earth gulp them down? The storm of that night washed away my entire family in one fleeting moment.

Throughout the night, the sound of loud wailings or suppressed sobs echoed throughout the house. Underneath those wailing cries and bitter sobs that particular fear that had been coiled around our hearts like a vicious snake seemed to be lost. For long it was slithering through our veins spreading fear and terror, but now, with its departure, all that was left in the house was nothing less than a deep, dark, gruesome cemetery-like situation.

I could feel Zosia's voice was coming from the deepest pit of some dark grave. I rose from my place and filled a glass with water from the nearby table and handed it to her. Zosia took a sip of water, stared at me, and took a deep breath.

"Are you ready to endure the pain of the events I am going to narrate now? Listen, I don't want you to lose all trust in humanity. Unfortunately, I lost all trust in mankind at a very tender age. But at the same time, I don't want you to be unaware of the animalistic traits of the so-called human beings that stay in the human system like dormant DNA and proliferate like cancer in the given situation and devour the last drop of humanity from its soul. Never ever form a one-sided view about them and receive the shock of your life when you least expect it because whatever happened to me in the past did not shock me or make me sad, but yes it did fill me with immense anger and hatred.

Saying this, Zosia inhaled deeply and I saw her eyes harden thinking of some harsh past event.

At that particular moment, for the first time, I saw in someone's eyes the simmering volcano of the past and the cold glacial of the present come together at once. I could see that the painful memories of the past were making it difficult for her to breathe, but she was still adamant about baring herself open.

I wanted to ease her burden; my only wish at that time was to rescue her from the suffocation she felt. I stared at the wrinkled expressionless face of Zosia for a long time and wondered if the next destination of aging is wrinkles then is maturity all about escaping the emotions and feelings that come with wrinkles?

I took the empty glass from her hands and put it back on the table. Once again I sat next to her and entered the bleak memories of her past that were filled with darkness and pain alone.

The terrible night was already gone, but at that time, I didn't know that the morning would be darker than the black night.

Before we could leave our house and go out in search of Papa and Uncle Josef, the broken door of our house shattered to the grounds with a loud explosion and dozens of German soldiers entered our house shouting and roaring loudly in their menacing voices. I had no clue as to why exactly they were shouting at us. Yes, I do remember vividly that I was clinging to my mother and wailing loudly and Jacob and Aidan stuck to Aunt Rebecca timidly. The soldiers began to throw out our belongings mercilessly. Everything they could get hold of in their fury was seen lying on the road next. Before I could realize what hit me, a huge giant-like hand grabbed me by my arms, snatched me away from my mother's chest, and threw me out of the house just like the rest of the objects. For a moment, I was up in the air, and for a while, I didn't know what was happening to me. Yes, before losing consciousness I could hear the heart-wrenching cries of Jacob and Aidan. The last I saw of them was their heads being bludgeoned by the butt of machine guns and boots.

I opened my eyes in a dark alley clutched against the bosom of my mother who was running frantically through the unknown lanes and by-lanes of the ghetto. There was only dust and smoke all around us. My mother was beyond herself with fear. But at that time, she didn't have anything else but to run for our lives. She was drenched in blood and sweat. Mama was running like a meek deer trying to save herself and me from those wild hounds. But then there was a heart-searing shriek and I could feel once again that I slipped from her frail chest and fragile arms and leaped in the air. Once again I crashed to the ground with a loud thud.

When my body crashed on the ground, it slipped and skidded and stuck at the corner without any chance of further movement. Alas! I so wished I was dead there and then or lost my consciousness that very moment. I wished I could have been anywhere else at that time in any condition. I would have preferred death over what I witnessed next lying on the floor. At that moment my heart was filled with an immortal hatred for mankind. My mother was lying in a corner with her dress torn in all the wrong places, her body badly battered and bruised with blood flowing from her open wounds. She was sobbing helplessly, more out of the torture of her soul than the physical pain. There was a truck of Nazi soldiers in front of her and it was a collision with that truck that caused the great fall in every sense of the word. They were a lot in number and my mother was just one. They were hungry wolves and my mother was their only meal. They devoured her like starving hyenas and my mother's limp body remained there oblivious to their cannibalistic acts. I had no clue as to why they were doing all this; first, they satiated their carnal hunger with her lifeless body and then all of them peed all over her face. God knows if my mama was dead or alive, but surely she was smeared in their filth.

The entire episode happened right in front of my eyes and burned my soul down to the ashes. I so wished I could have died that day! Wished that wrath from the sky befell on Earth. Wished! The earth split open on that day and all of us were lost in the darkness of the blank space. I hoped and wished the entire universe would come crashing down upon us and annihilate the entirety of mankind. But nothing of the sort happened. I lived. And so did my mother. The sky remained erect in its place and stared at everything shamelessly. And the earth didn't act any differently; she too looked at us in the same shameless manner.

After a while, the Nazi truck left and the lane was filled with utter silence. My mother, in the middle of the road, covered in filth and blood, lay lifelessly. I sobbed sitting in the corner. Someone in a house nearby opened the window and a nervous woman came out looking scared with a large piece of cloth in her hand. She looked

41

here and there and then ran towards my mother. She covered her naked body with that cloth. Gradually, a few people sneaked out of their homes scared and gathered around my mother. Together, all of them lifted her and took her inside a house next door. They also lifted me from the corner and laid me next to Mama in the corner. My mother in her semi-unconsciousness lay next to me like some clock that was just ticking without moving an inch. Blood oozed from various parts of her body and the pungent smell of urine wafted from her. A woman cleaned her body with a wet cloth. She wrapped her in a blanket and sat silently in the corner. I have no idea when exactly I slept or slipped into unconsciousness. I opened my eyes to an entirely different world.

$$\blacklozenge$$

I don't know how exactly I reached there, but all I remember is it was a long train filled with too many men, women, and children. I had no idea where exactly it was going, maybe Germany, or maybe some other city in Poland or maybe to a particular place where all these passengers were destined to reach. I was starving and felt extremely cold. Everybody was starving on that train or rather all of us were malnourished. Our stomachs stuck to our backs and ribs protruded out. Their faces were devoid of all colors and their eyes were dry. Suddenly, I felt cramps in my abdomen; I wanted to scream, but instead of any sound coming out of my mouth I felt bile sliding down my throat. With great difficulty, I pulled my frail hands and placed them on my stomach. My whole body felt numb. The chugging sound of the train was the only sign of life on it.

Many of the passengers were in near-to-deathlike conditions whereas some were partially alive just like me. Their irregular breathing was very similar to the train sound; instead of following a straight path, it ambled and juggled from left to right, heavy to slow. Some of them had their eyes closed while many were stretched flat on their back or stomachs staring at either the train ceiling or its shivering floor. I don't remember whether I thought of my parents at that time or not, but for a brief moment I thought of Jacob and Aidan hoping that maybe they too were here. I also tried to look at a few 10–12-year-old kids trying to locate Jacob and Aidan among them. There was no sign of them. I hoped they were there. But then Aunt Rebecca and Uncle Josef too were missing.

Once again, I clutched my abdomen. I don't know whether I crashed into a slumber or lost consciousness due to the benumbing pain.

———————◆———————

Zosia took a deep breath and stared into the distance for some time as if she was trying to recall something. I myself was traveling with her in that ill-fated train on that fateful journey to nowhere land. Her deep breath pulled me out of that train and brought me to the middle of her living room. I could see her eyes were still dry and devoid of any feelings, quite similar to those passengers traveling with her on that train. But I wanted to stay on that train a little longer. I eagerly waited for its next station. However, it was not as important to her anymore as it was for me. Maybe it was mainly because of the fact that she already knew what the next pages of her diary contained.

"Are you alright, Zosia?" I asked her gently. She blinked and ignored my question.

"I don't know how Mama died. I always wonder. It is a fact, though, that she died that very moment in the middle of the road that night

43

when she was debased, defiled, and humiliated by a Nazi battalion, but the thought still haunts me."

"Did you ever come to know what exactly happened to your father, Aunt Rebecca, Uncle Josef, or Jacob and Aidan?" I once again looked at her and put forward my question as gently as I could.

"The same that happened to other Polish people at the hands of German soldiers," Zosia muttered under her breath.

She stared at the carpet for some time, and then I don't what exactly she was thinking. I saw her close the diary and place it on the table. And then she raised her eyes and looked at me. "My heart feels very heavy; can we continue this meeting some other day?"

"Sure, sure why not?" I replied instantly. "I can understand how difficult it must have been for you to go back and relive those nightmares one more time. Moreover, you are doing all this for me alone, I am extremely grateful."

"I don't know, but yes this is a tedious task because this diary is more of a memoir created out of memories, which is why many of my life events are lost in these pages," Zosia replied in the same frail voice.

"Okay, I will leave now," I said, rising from the couch and moving a little closer to her. I planted a soft kiss on her cheek. "Please get some rest now. I will call you soon and we will sit once again."

"Oh my! I didn't even offer you tea or coffee today," she said, realizing it all of a sudden.

"Never mind, next time." Saying this I left her house.

While driving the car I could hear my heartbeat continuously and felt queasy for some unknown reason.

CHAPTER 5

When I returned home, everything was exactly the same. Nothing had changed.

The very same pin drop silence that was crying to break free with the sound of my footsteps. The way the same darkness pined to get lit up by the mere flicker of my fingers. The very same depression that lived in the prison of embracing happiness someday. And the same feeling of an unmoving time where hours turned into minutes and minutes into seconds with each tick of the needle. Neither did the sound of my footsteps break the silence nor did my fingers extinguish the darkness within when I turned the lights on. My arrival did not transform the depression into a state of happiness. Last but not the least, the ticking needle did not bring a drop of change in the present time. I took off my sandals at the doorstep and then placed my purse on the table. I went to the fridge in the kitchen and got hold of a cold bottle of water. Holding the bottle in my hands, I did not pour it into a glass; instead, I drank from it directly without touching the bottle with my mouth. I poured the cold water directly into my mouth thinking the water would pass through my parched lips and dry mouth and quench years of thirst. I thought the water would act like a balm and help me feel fresh and alive again.

Then I went to my room from the kitchen, and lying on the bed I stared at the ceiling silently. All my thoughts were lost somewhere, my mind had kind of become numb and my body felt slightly weak and frail, but I had a feeling all these things did not happen overnight or all of a sudden. When I sat with Zosia listening to the pages of her life story, at that time, I felt that Fatma was getting transformed into the characters that belonged to Zosia's life. I was no longer myself or rather my old self.

At times, I turned into Zosia's papa whereas, at other times, I felt I was her mama. In those few hours, I turned into everybody that was once a part of Zosia's life. I was everyone she came across. I was her Uncle Josef and Aunt Rebecca, her cousins Jacob and Aidan, and then there were times when I felt I was Zosia herself.

While listening to her story, I smelled the filth and audacious odor of the Nazi soldiers and found my body smeared in their urine and sperm just like Zosia's mother. I saw the bullets from their machine guns hole my body like her papa and Uncle Josef, and I also felt the pain of Jacob and Aidan when the heavy boots and butts of the guns of uniformed demons smashed their frail heads and bodies.

Today, I was looking at the ruins with the eyes of Papa and Uncle Josef, the darkness that engulfed the lives of Zosia's mama and Aunt Rebecca, and covered in the blood of Aidan and Jacob, I returned to my place.

Did I return or was I lost somewhere there? I thought.

What was this discomfort I had returned with? Something that a mere few pages from Zosia's diary inserted in me.

What was this fear that spread far and wide within me? I could feel this fear under my skin right through my fingertips. Maybe it was this fear, anxiety, and sheer apprehension I felt that benumbed me and made my body turn lifeless. Not in my wildest dreams did I imagine that my quest for the missing pages of Zosia Casnova's life would turn my world upside down. I had no idea that the dust and dirt of the very same lost pages would rub off on me so viciously. Without a word, I continued to stare at the ceiling. Alone and lonely, my only companion was the tick-tock sound of the wall clock in my room; its sound merged with that of my heartbeat and it reverberated through my ears and convinced me of my existence.

Yes, I was alive, but was I alive or merely existing? Lost in these thoughts I closed my eyes, and then, in no time, the chaos and claustrophobia of the train of Zosia's life screamed within me and I sat bolt upright. The pictures of her life that I clicked on with my mind's eye and felt so disturbed about were a part and parcel of Zosia's album. And she had lived through every inch of it. Unable to take it anymore, I left the bed and went outside. The lane outside was as isolated as the room was silent. I had no clue whether this silence entered my body from the outside or if it was the silence within that spread outside and quieted everything around me. I had to break the silence I decided anxiously and then feared that this silence might devour me completely.

Something needs to be done to break the silence, I thought. *I should go to some mall and indulge in window shopping or I should simply go to Atya, I am sure her vibrant company would help me get out of this depressing environment.* Returning to the bedroom, I looked at myself in the dressing table mirror, my face looked tired. I applied a little compact powder on my face and ran my fingers through my hair and tied it into a bun and clasped it with a hair catcher. Turning around, I lifted my bag, and then, sitting on the chair, I began to tie the straps of my sandals. Rising from the chair I went out of the house and took out the bunch of keys from my bag; I locked the door and then, carrying the car keys and house keys in my hand, I went down the stairs.

While driving, I thought instead of going to the shopping mall, it would be better if I should go to Atya's place. Her stupid little jokes and silly gossip would surely lighten my mood.

"Hello, Atya, I am coming your way," I informed her over the phone.

"Definitely, I am home, come fast." Her reply was light and happy as always.

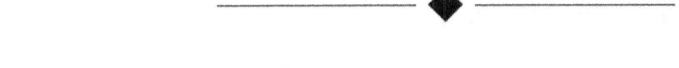

Doctor Sahab was also present in the house. Atya straightaway dragged me to the dining table and forced me to have dinner with them. Atya's husband was a renowned psychiatrist and was extremely fun to be with. Even at small things, he laughed heartily. No sooner did he see me than he said, "Hey Journalist Ma'am, welcome, welcome." He always addressed me as Journalist Ma'am. However, the only connection I had with journalism was that I worked in a private news agency whose job it was to prepare news and information for TV, radio, and other media channels. I spent most of the time engrossed in writing and editing content for them.

With great difficulty, I forced a smile at Atya's husband and said, "How is everything, Doctor Sahab?" My mood hadn't changed much. I was still feeling the same.

"I am absolutely fine, but you don't look so good yourself." It seemed as though just a glance had made him realize the inner turmoil I was going through. "Is everything okay?"

Atya also readily added, "Oh yes, you look a little worried, is it because of the heat outside?"

At that very moment, Doctor Sahab said, "Or is it because of the cold climate within? Looks like our journalist is badly missing Asad." This time Doctor Sahab sounded a little serious.

Before I could open my mouth to say anything, Atya stopped me. "Well, our Fatma always misses Asad, don't you?"

She looked at me mischievously.

At that time, I decided to keep the topic light because my mood was already screwed.

"Yeah man, I can say that that gentleman there is roaming around Kashmir and all I have here are his nagging memories."

"Hey, Kashmir reminds me, the Indians over there are oppressing the innocent Kashmiris. What do you have to say about it?"

I was trying to evade all things political and here I was, surrounded by talk of political issues. Trying to shun the topic, I said, "Doctor Sahab, I have no clue, there are three different ideologies. The Indian government has its own point of view and Pakistan has its own, but my vote is for the common people of Kashmir because to me they are of utmost importance and best aware of their problem. The main problem is the intelligence agencies of both countries are hell-bent on establishing their own agenda. And amongst all this, different news regarding the valley is reaching the sky so that the citizens of both India and Pakistan are trapped in the propaganda mission or media trap and view the problems from the eyes of their own rulers and stay far away from reality." Without any motive or intention I spoke my heart out in one single breath.

Doctor Sahab silently signaled Atya to pass the bowl of curry; Atya offered it to me first and said, "Alright, take something first and leave aside all these big talks and tell me did you eat your lunch or not or are simply surviving on breakfast in the morning?"

I ladled some curry onto my plate and passed on the bowl to Doctor Sahab.

"Umm ... the food is delicious," I said, looking at her.

"Man! There is magic in her hands, I am not crazy about her just for her looks," the doctor said jovially.

"Hey, with you saying 'crazy' I remember." Suddenly, without giving a second thought to it, I asked him abruptly, "What is the final face (phase) of craziness?"

"Oh my God! Such a serious question, Journalist Ma'am. Is everything alright? I thought you would ask me about the final stage of love?"

Once again, he applied psychological tactics to lighten the situation.

"Alright, in answer to that...." This time Atya also accompanied Doctor Sahab in lightening the mood further. "Well, I feel the final destination of love is madness, the way our doctor of the mentally ill patients lost his marbles after falling in love with me and is also a prisoner of my soul."

With the naughty way in which Atya raised her eyebrows all the heaviness within me vanished for a minute and a smile spread across my face.

"Atya is absolutely right on this," Doctor Sahab said, taking a bite of his flatbread.

"Atya love, my stomach is full but I am not. Kindly bring in some dessert; you know post meal without dessert…."

And then Atya completed Doctor Sahab's rhetoric. "Life doesn't feel sweet."

No sooner did Atya rise from the dining table and head towards the kitchen to get desserts for Doctor Sahab than he looked at me seriously and asked in a grave tone, "By the way, is everything fine? Why are you drifting towards the final stage of madness?"

"No, I am not talking about myself, my situation has not reached that point yet," I replied with a smile.

"Well, in my opinion, madness itself is the final stage of life; beyond madness life loses all reason and rationality." Doctor Sahab was trying his best to avoid talking about death at the dining table or so I felt on listening to his theory. When I thought of death, I also realized that Zosia had pulled herself from the final stage of madness and escaped to life. What would have been her catharsis? After all, how did she manage to keep herself alive and protect herself from madness? To know everything about Zosia Casnova was of prime importance to me.

Up until now, I had been trying to reach her or know about her only to learn more about myself, but after today's meeting to unravel the confusing layers of life….

I was lost in my own thoughts; suddenly Atya's voice against my ears woke me up from my reverie. "Hello."

I was back at the dining table one more time and started to serve some dessert on my plate from the bowl offered by Atya.

All of us retired to the living room after dinner.

Once we were seated comfortably, Doctor Sahab, looking at Atya, requested, "Dear, can we have one round of tea, please? I will just go change into something comfortable." He was referring to his suit and tie.

"Tell me, how is everything else?" Atya smiled at me as she sat next to me on the sofa.

"Nothing much, I was just thinking of going to Dhaka for a few days," I blurted unintentionally. I was only thinking about it, I don't know how I said it out loud.

"Wow! All of a sudden. How come?" Atya was clearly taken by surprise. "When we met a few days ago, you didn't tell me anything about going to Dhaka or any such plans."

"Well, to be honest, this is something I decided just now," I replied with all honesty.

"Is it something important or are you going just like that?" Atya asked and then continued, "Hey, what about your meeting with that lady whatshername, yeah, Zosia Casnova? How did it go?" There was a fleeting sign of curiosity on Atya's face, which vanished as soon as it appeared.

"Of course, I will tell you. We discussed only a little stuff. I will share everything with you once I know her entire story. As of now, all I can say is that Zosia is not just a woman but an entire history on her own." I tried to explain the situation to Atya as precisely as I could.

"Alright, no problem, but you need to tell me what is this thing about Dhaka? I don't remember you ever returning to Bangladesh since your childhood. How old were you when you came here with your mother?"

"Maybe two. Well, this is what Ammi told me. I vaguely remember I used to wander one after another locality holding my Ammi's finger. It was the time when the two of us were trying to locate our distant relatives here in Karachi. Those were extremely difficult days, Ammi used to walk with torn slippers and she used to walk in this manner for hours. Sometimes, she carried me in her arms, while at other times, she held my finger," I replied, lost in the days gone by.

"Post that, your mother also never returned?" Atya asked, rising from the couch. "Let's go to the kitchen, we will talk there as I make tea."

"I remember maybe she went there a couple of times," I said as I rose from the couch to join her, "maybe when her mother died. Yes, she also told me once that she had some relatives or maybe cousins who often called her. Atya, she really faced extremely difficult times here. She used to work as a house help in so many homes and raised me by giving me a decent education. Poor thing, tough luck; when I came of age, she passed away. She had a very sad life. I never saw her smile or laugh heartily. Ammi never enjoyed any luxury or comfort."

Atya looked at me sympathetically and then within an instant she changed her expression. "Leave it, yeah? Let bygones be bygones. What's done is done; we can't do anything about it now. But her wish to give you good education got fulfilled, didn't it? Look at you, you are doing so well in your career and your life is also nice and comfortable. Now all we need is for you to get married to Asad. Come on man, you need to settle down and start a family." She smiled mischievously to change my mood.

"Bro, but one thing always nags me—why did Ammi leave Bangladesh and come to Karachi when her entire family was there only? In fact, she never told me a thing about my Abbu. I asked her so many times, but she always evaded the topic one way or another. Honestly speaking, I don't know who my father is. She didn't even show his picture to me. Not once. Whenever I asked her anything, her only reply was, 'He died in an accident.' She used to say that all his photographs were left behind in Bangladesh and then everything got lost. But then what are these things written in her diary, and those pics of a European kid, what is all that? Isn't it hard to believe that she could carry a diary all the way from Bangladesh to Karachi but not my father's pictures? Girls are crazy about their wedding albums, photographs, memories, and mementos; they treasure them all and keep them close. So how come she didn't bring any such thing with her? I always felt she was hiding something from me.

Suddenly, the steam in the kettle made a whistling sound. Atya turned off the switch and poured the tea into cups. Atya carried her and Doctor Sahab's cups and I carried my own and both of us returned to the living room.

Doctor Sahab had changed his clothes and was browsing through one of his medical magazines. He took his cup from Atya and returned to the couch again. Placing the magazine back on the table, he turned to me and asked, "Tell me more, Journalist Ma'am, what's new? How is your friend Asad?"

"Well, Fatma is planning to go to Bangladesh," Atya informed him.

"Okayyy." Doctor Sahab stretched his okay a bit longer than was necessary. "Well, that's great news. After all, it is your motherland," he said, looking at me. "Do you still have relatives there?"

"No, Doctor Sahab," I replied, taking a small sip from my cup. "As far as my knowledge goes, I don't think I have any relatives there, plus Ammi never told me anything of the sort."

"Aha! So you are going there just for a change. Well, I would suggest you should definitely go, and why only Bangladesh? I suggest you visit other countries as well. Do you know traveling is great for mental health? New destinations, travel attractions, and a whole new culture and traditions, what more could you ask for? You must go and stay there for some time. Is Asad also going with you?" Doctor Sahab asked.

"Doctor Sahab, I have just thought of it and you've chalked up the entire plan," I told him with a smile. "Asad has no clue about it. I only shared a thought with Atya that I am tired of leading a routine and monotonous life. I need a change. Hence, this is the only reason why I thought of going to Bangladesh and, as you said, taking a look at my MOTHERLAND," I repeated after him.

"I also feel that you shouldn't go to Bangladesh all by yourself. If possible both you and Asad must go together, so that you can enjoy your time." Atya came up with a romantic idea as usual.

"Good lord! You are too much, sweetheart, I am not planning a honeymoon. Okay, leave it. Tell me, Doctor Sahab, is marriage good for mental health or extremely injurious?" I asked Doctor Sahab humorously, placing the empty cup on the table.

Doctor Sahab gave out a hearty laugh. "This reminds me of a song, *Tum itna jo muskura rahey ho, kya gham hai jisko chhupa rahey ho.*"

Atya also laughed. "Come on, Doctor Sahab, let it be, you too are a total nutcase. This is not a song but actually a poem by Kaifi Azmi." Then she added, "Kaifi Azmi must be rolling in his grave listening to his poem being butchered so badly."

This made me laugh uncontrollably and Doctor Sahab too couldn't help but laugh at Atya's antics.

Later that night, while returning home, I thought it was high-time Asad and I should get married. It was not that injurious to mental health.

CHAPTER 6

By the time I reached home, it was quite late at night. The next morning, I had to go to my job as well; hence I decided to hit the sack straight away, but then I changed my mind and turned on my laptop with the sole purpose of checking e-mails. There was Asad's love mail! The more I read it the deeper I got into the world of Asad, leaving my own way behind. Asad had opened his heart to me with total love. He composed his love letter by combining a poem of Joseph Berowski and the situation in Kashmir.

Fatma,
Wish you were here, love
Wish you were here
Wish you were seated here on this sofa
And I was next to you
Your scarf,
And my tears, restrained to my face
If this was possible, for sure
Its reverse as well

Wish you were here, love
wish you were here
Wish we were together, in our car
And you would have changed the gear

We would have found ourselves somewhere else
On an unknown shore
And would have changed ourselves
Where we once belonged

Wish you were here, love
Wish you were here
wish I didn't have the knowledge of the stars
When the stars appear
When the moon reflects on the water
It turns half asleep and takes a deep sigh
Hope! It remained like a quarter only
So would have dialed your number
Wish you were here, love
Secluded in isolation
Me sitting on the patio
Sipping cold beer
It's evening, the sun is about to set
The boys are screaming and the girls are crying
What's the importance of forgetting
If it is followed by death alone?
Fatma!

You are right; no more am I your poet boyfriend, the one who
cajoled you with Tagore's poems. Now I live like an old man
clinging to your thoughts with the hope that I will get to know the
meaning of life. What shall I do, Fatma? Staying apart from you has
filled me with delusion and despair. You are correct; I am actually
losing my poetic self, but you must compliment me because despite
all the negativity and calamities, I am still holding myself strong. I
am alive with all my might. Fatma, you run through my veins like
blood and your thoughts flow through my broken heart like tears of
hopelessness. But it is a fact that this prison of confinement has

filled me with such intense pain that now I find you inseparable. I am with you all the time even though we are far apart. Tell you something, the things that I see around me on a daily basis have deprived me of my own self. They have pushed me to the limits of questioning my own faith. I have no clue what is this war that I am fighting. Fatma, I am breaking from inside, blood is oozing from my open wounds. At times, I feel I have left myself far behind, I am just running aimlessly to save a shallow self.

Fatma, it is your love, the poems of Tagore, and the warmth of our skin that has sustained me up until now. Let not my broken heart worry you. If I want, I can leave all this instantly and stand right next to you, but I want to reach the destination of love. I want to reach life by passing through life. Emotions and poems alone cannot make me realize the vivid reality of this torment, oppression, fascism, and fear. To reach my goal, I need to pass through hope and hopelessness. I want to return to you like a soldier. I will return to you very soon, Fatma. So soon that you too will be surprised. Hey, you wrote or rather asked me if I remember you. Now, tell me how am I supposed to forget you? I remember everything; I remember your soft, bright, innocent face. Your intoxicating brooding eyes and your pleasant personality. That carelessness. Each and every thing is deeply sketched in my heart.

I also remember that morning when I saw you for the first time in college. You followed your mother nervously with your eyes cast down taking meticulously careful steps. I also remember that afternoon when you stood on the stage with four of your friends and spoke vociferously about women's rights. Yes, I also remember that evening when we went out for the first time, when we took our vows to live and die together. And then maybe I don't remember a single day during those four years when I didn't talk to you. It was nearly impossible to pass a day without getting a glimpse of you. I also remember each and every day of these two years ever since I came here. I am spending morning, noon, and night without you. My condition is quite like this.

It was only after getting separated from you that I realized

You were not just you but you carried my entire world inside you.

If I had got a job in Karachi, I would never have come here, you know it way too well, as I do. Yes, I know you have got a job and had I stayed there a little longer I too would have got something and would have never had to leave you, but you know it don't you? Not even in my wildest dreams did I know life would test me so crucially. I feel, in a way, this new journey is not that bad; it is very good indeed because all the ideologies and theories I used to discuss and debate with you nature proposed a practical opportunity to me so that I can get a first-hand experience of all my ideals. How these Kashmiris are paying a heavy price for the politics between India and Pakistan. I am in a new world, a world that is in stark contrast to my romantic world, it is horrifying and scary. In this new world, youths are dying every day, kids are blinded and women are debased and defamed. My condition is such that every day I create a new God and every day this God gets shattered into tiny little pieces.

The humanity I was once proud of, in reality, is weaker and frailer than my dreams.

Yesterday, I bumped into this poem by some anonymous poet. I could relate to it so closely. I felt it is actually my voice.

To date I couldn't master the skill of pottery
For eternity I have been kneading the dough with tears
Nothing could appear in my sight
It is just an imagination

Just a faint imagination
An imagination that doesn't fit into any image
I feel a sketch doodling within me
No idea who is crying within me
Tears are rolling down my face
Within me lies a cold self, resident of the deep ocean
Nothing can be seen
The oil in the night lamp is burning out
For eternity I have been kneading the dough with tears
To date, I couldn't master the skill of pottery

Fatma, I will take my leave now, in the morning I have to report to I.S.P.R. that the Indians have devised a new technique to combat the armed rebels. In the meantime, they have kept 20 villagers as hostages, each and every house is searched, and the people are being brutally beaten. The rulers in New Delhi have accused our people from Islamabad of spreading extremism in their land. I am to investigate everything and prepare a report. I was thinking while submitting the report, should I add this couplet by Muneer Niazi? Anyway, they don't really know that there lies a poet behind this uniformed soldier, the heart of a human being.

Futile and fruitless, war and peace, rise and fall
All the victories are the same and all the defeats are alike
Now none have the dedication of the days gone by
All the tribes are the same, all the castes are alike

I take leave with the promise to meet you again for eternity.

Always yours,
Asad

CHAPTER 7

The next morning, while working in the office, I don't know what came over me, I dialed Bangladesh Embassy. There I came to know it was not very difficult to avail myself of a visit visa, especially for someone like me who was born in Bangladesh. It filled me with great happiness that due to my birth in Bangladesh it would be easier for me to get the visa. Before my admission to a school, my mother had changed her citizenship and I too had turned into a Pakistani citizen along with her. On hearing about the online visa application, I heaved a sigh of relief because standing in queues is something I despised. No sooner had I put the phone back in its cradle than it began to scream loudly, it felt as if I didn't place it on a cradle but attached it to some musical instrument. Picking up the phone, I said hello.

There was Zosia on the other end. "Hello Fatma." Her voice seemed to be coming from some bottomless pit. "My girl, can you quickly come to me?" she pleaded.

"Yes, of course, I will be right there," I tried to console her and also added, "To be honest, even if you didn't call me today I was planning to give you a call—"

"Why are you sounding so formal today? Is there some sort of distance between us now?" She interrupted me midway, seemingly taken aback by my response.

"Well, nothing of the sort, the moment you called me 'My girl,' I automatically addressed you in the manner I used to address my mother," I replied with a smile on my face.

"Come on, Fatma, don't be so formal, you know Western people don't depend much on formality while addressing someone older than them. To you, it may be a sign of respect, but to us, respect is not restricted to the way you address a person but the way you treat a person. Words are just a medium to express your feelings. Never mind, it's really bad that I always drift away from the main subject. You are free to address me the way you deem fit. Whatever makes you happy makes me happy too.

"So where were we?" Zosia once again tried to get back to the sentence that was interrupted by her midway.

"Well, I was trying to say that had you not called me today I would have surely dialed your number and sought an appointment with you."

"Oh!" Zosia inhaled softly and told me in a lost voice, "Well, I don't have anything else to give you except my time."

"In that case, consider yourself extremely lucky because people have everything in this world except for that one particular thing. And trust me, time is definitely the most priceless thing we have in our lives." I tried to add extra vigor to my voice and make her feel enthusiastic.

"Fatma, you are an amazing girl. You know how to make people feel happy," Zosia said happily.

"Alright then, tell me when do I drop in?" I asked her humorously.

"Whenever you wish, just make sure to make it quick." The appeal was evident in her voice. I could feel she was burdened with loneliness.

"I will make sure I meet you as soon as possible; in fact, this time I wish to spend some quality time with you in a restaurant or somewhere out in the open so that we are away from the drab environment of closed doors." I took another step towards making our friendship stronger.

"Sure, sure, why not? There is a very nice park quite near my place and a few decent restaurants. This is a very good idea indeed. I too want to get out of the stuffy surroundings of my home. Fatma, I will wait for you."

"Absolutely." I hung up after saying goodbye.

After putting the phone back in its place, I continued to stare at it. For some time, the web of my thoughts spun around the life of Zosia, and then, after some time, I began to untangle myself from this web, and soon I was away from thoughts of Zosia and back at my desk. I turned on my laptop and checked those columns on our company's website that had arrived to me in the past 24 hours from different newspapers. The majority of the columns that were politically based where the authors discussed and put forward their views on national and international political issues; some were based on social issues, women's empowerment, sexual molestation of children and some also expressed their discomfort about ever-increasing street crimes. One after another I pasted those columns into my company's website after properly editing them.

In no time, my fingers and the keyboard got accustomed to each other and were totally in sync. My gaze was fixed on the laptop screen and it was all I could see at that time. I read rows after rows of columns given to me and continued to edit and rectify grammatical errors, adjusting the alignment of sentences and paragraphs. Everything was running so smoothly, but suddenly I realized something was not right. I realized I had edited the grammar, sentences, paragraphs, and content of the columns but I was simply unable to go into the very depths of the content, I was not able to connect with it. This thought made me slow down my pace and in no time the laptop screen, alphabet on the keyboard, and I could feel the three of us finally forming a perfect sync with one another. I realized this column was written in such a manner that required a different sort of editing from me. One such editing that was not connected to my typing fingers, keyboard alphabets, its paragraphs, or grammatical errors related to it but called for a human touch. It needed to be connected to my heartbeats and emotions contained within, it was connected to my blinking eyes and my sight; it did not require connection with my rational mind but to my ideas and imaginations of life.

For a while, I stopped my fingers from typing right there and took a long breath and began to read the column one more time. It was not a column but a wailing that cried about the oppressions and torments of the Indian police and paramilitary force on the innocent Kashmiri civilians. It spoke of the horrors of shooting teargas and shotguns at close range over the unarmed protestors in the Valley of Kashmir and also the application of pellet guns and bird shotguns at point-blank range. I found myself in the open sky of the Valley of Kashmir; every time birds stretched their wings to fly high, at that very moment bullets from the bird shotguns began to rain on them bringing them down to the ground writhing and convulsing in great pain. And then, in order to save their lives, they ran frantically on the streets of the valley, colliding with each other, falling to the ground, screaming in agony; covering their eyes with two hands they ran around like crazy just to save their lives. Unfortunately, these were not mere birds, they were the ordinary people of Kashmir who were born free like any other bird, to fly and to soar freely, but their flights were restricted, the movement of their wings was predetermined, and the colorful light in their eyes was filled with pitch-black darkness.

As I proceeded with my editing I could feel one after another nest forming inside my chest and then getting shattered one by one. The birds peeping from these nests were scared, their delicate wings quivered with fear and their eyes, injured by pellet guns, oozed blood.

I shut down the laptop screen abruptly and made my back touch the chair. Resting my head against the back of the chair I looked up and stared at the ceiling of our office silently. I wondered which power it was that compelled a few people to shoot at other people at the mere call of the word FIRE!

CHAPTER 8

The next day, after leaving the office, when I went to meet Zosia at her place, I could see she was ready to go out with me.

She had brushed her silvery white hair in such a manner that it had kind of curled around her ears from both sides; in spite of this, a black stone studded in a gold ring peeked from the veil of her white hair. Old age and experience had etched her forehead with all kinds of lines, which also covered her chin and went down to her neck, but even now her rose-tinted cheeks and sharp nose were devoid of any wrinkles or signs of old age. I could see Zosia did not apply any lipstick, but her naturally beautiful well-shaped lips stood out and hinted at her timeless beauty. She had donned a thin blue cardigan that rested around the thin gold necklace on her neck, making her refined personality look classier. The moment she saw me she said, "I have been ready since noon; after a long, long time I am going out with someone, which is why I am feeling a little excited today."

"I too feel the same." I smiled and replied to her in all honesty.

"Hey, listen, you have come right from your office, you can use the washroom if you so wish and freshen up. As it's just five p.m. now, at this time the restaurants and cafés will be nearly vacant.

Normally, people in Karachi take dinner after eight o'clock whereas we Europeans get done with our dinner at six thirty only. By the way, I hope you didn't have your dinner, did you? Tonight, we are going to have our dinner together." Zosia was unstoppable that day; she chalked out the entire plan in one single breath. This made me realize Zosia was actually desperately craving to go out of her house. "I am all set to leave, please lock the door."

Moving back a little I gave her some space so that she could leave the house. I could see that she carried her walking stick that was resting against the side of the door. Handing the walking stick to me, she bent over to lock the door. Suddenly, the thought of her diary came to my mind, but before I could say anything, she began to grumble something under her breath.

"Don't worry; the diary is inside my bag." Locking the gate she placed the keys inside a small leather pouch and dropped it inside a bag that hung around her arm. I handed her back the stick; she stated as she took the stick from me, "I am over seventy-five now, but thankfully I use it only to feel the support."

Feeling genuinely impressed, I thought, *Zosia is really a woman with an incredible spirit and immense physical strength who endured great calamities and faced great difficulties. She has been fighting an ominous battle all her life with absolute courage and valor.*

When we reached the road, while sitting in the car she said, "Just near Phase Six there is Bukhari Park, if you drive on this road for five to ten minutes you will come across many authentic Chinese restaurants."

"Sure." I started the car and pushed the accelerator with my feet slowly, very slowly.

Soon the two of us were sitting in an authentic Chinese restaurant against a giant glass window through which the whole of the street outside was visible. Right in the middle of the road, there was a tiny pavement that stretched at a lengthy distance carrying Conocarpus plants on either side with the sporadic intrusion of banyan, coconut, and neem trees every now and then. There were also a few giant banyan trees on the road that created a cool tarpaulin for the pedestrians and provided soothing shade and a cool breeze to anyone who walked under it. Behind these trees, there were some huge buildings, or some malls, and a few four–six-story plazas that were guarded by security personnel who were seen busily talking to one another. After finishing the dinner, I offered Zosia tea, which she declined, and she began looking for the diary inside her bag.

"Everything mentioned in these pages was either written instantaneously or retained through memory. Now, due to old age, very few events are left in my memory, and whatever you see in these pages will look like incidents of a previous life." While talking, Zosia opened her diary from the middle and then with her palm she smoothened out a folded page from the diary. She said, "Alright, I was telling you about me in a train that was full of people, the majority of whom were sick or unwell, and many were weak and fragile, their eyes were dry, and their bellies stuck to their backs. Maybe they had been starving for a long time and were also without a drop of water. But they were too many, so great was their number that the train seemed to appear small and narrow as they crammed every inch of it with their lifeless selves."

After reading it, Zosia lifted her eyes from the page, and for some time her blue eyes behind those wrinkled lids stared deep into my eyes. In that one moment, I realized as if centuries swam from her eyes into mine. The centuries that flowed drop by drop like an incessant rain, the rows after rows of water droplets that kissed the leaves and crashed onto the earth, flying up in the air, wandering aimlessly towards some unknown destination.

Then Zosia inhaled a deep breath and said, "Fatma, do you know what is untermensch?"

Before I could reply in negation, Zosia said, "Untermensch is a German term whose meaning is not known to God itself, most probably."

"What do you mean? I don't get it," I said in a very soft voice.

"Fatma, there are certain terms that have the capacity to consume humanity with the burning fire within them. They devour humanity over and over again. Untermensch is one such term, a term you too will be faced with in your life and witness its shameless dance of death. Listen to me my dear girl, if you ever witness this word then I suggest or rather request you to close your eyes and turn your head, don't look at it. Never ever let it enter your system else in no time, without having the slightest idea, you will transform into an animal. The human within you would die a silent death and be replaced by a vicious vengeful beast. Alright, leave all this as of now. Where was I?

"Yeah, I was telling you I was going on a train and during World War II it was the period of Germanisation. I came to know about all this later on, a few years had already passed and now I was a slightly grown-up girl. At that time, Hitler had vanquished a few other nations along with Poland, and like an autocratic ruler to annihilate the Jews, wherein too many children were also involved, they were dragged out of their ghettos and stuffed inside the train and sent over to the detention camps and prisons. The sole purpose of all this was mass genocide, an unimaginable holocaust or just to rehabilitate them into new societies as an inferior race or labor class so that their entire race would vanish like dust. As per Hitler all of us were just untermensch, which is why we were also pulled out of Warsaw and sent to Pazzo camp because in Warsaw the opposition was compelled to put an end to these detention camps."

Zosia lifted the diary closer to her eyes and began to read; I noticed the moment the words from her diary touched her lips and spread in the air, they took the form of a paintbrush and the window looked like an easel to me and everything outside the window slowly began to change form. The long stretch of the concrete road soon turned into a dusty narrow lane; the security guards hovering around the malls and plazas appeared like uniformed German soldiers who hit and pushed thousands of men, women, and children to form a straight line and walk in that long dusty lane. These poor people were pushed from all sides by rows and rows of German soldiers. The faces of the men were heavy and lifeless; I could see they had lost all hope. The tears had dried on the cheeks of women and children and their faces were not just streaked with tears that had dried out but fear too was etched all over their faces. I could feel all these people knew where they were headed to even before reaching there.

◆

I was just nine or 10 years old, but I was extremely scared of those buildings. They were not homes but were actually haunted houses. The ceilings, floors, walls even the gates were made up of wood. During the winters, these buildings turned into cold torture chambers. Each one of the rooms at a time housed six to eight individuals whereas its capacity was not sufficient to contain more than four people. People who lived there were not humans but ailing carcasses who stuck to one another from wall to wall and their only task was to wait for their death. Some of them were so weak that they couldn't stand up even after being given support. The detainees in those houses were fed once a day, which could barely suffice as a decent meal, the Nazis did this on purpose so that the Jewish prisoners would die a natural death there.

Too many rooms of the building were such where an entire family lived at once, for instance two to three females, a few males and children lived together. These families were ever so scared and always hid behind one another when they walked out. As it was they hardly left their rooms. One or two buildings were such that housed females only—females of all ages.

At times, when some men and women could not bear the monotony anymore, they used to become restless and run out of the house and pull the barbed wire with their bare hands and cry helplessly. During these situations, the Nazi soldiers retaliated by barking at them, and then, in no time, there occurred shootings and stampede-like situations ever so frequently. When the crowd scattered and everything got back to normal, next to the barbed wire dead bodies of women, children and men were found. But this was nothing new; it was a daily occurrence there and had been going on for years, way before my arrival. The people were brought in trains, pushed inside those camps, and after some time many of them were killed and many were sent to labor camps to work. The dead bodies were instantly lifted and dumped inside the trucks one on top of another and carried to the forests where huge pits were dug. These bodies were then buried in those trenches. Initially, when I first got there, I was taken aback by the sight of such looming prisons for the people wherein they were stuffed to die without any visible faults. Far and wide, they did not have any supporters or allies.

Within a few days only, I realized there are only two types of people in this world—one who are being killed and the other those who are given the task of killing, and for this, there is no animosity required. We didn't know one another at all because I could not understand one word of the language these soldiers spoke and maybe they too did not have any idea what we used to talk about among ourselves. They were of queer disposition, their feet sunk in huge military boots, tall with broad shoulders carrying guns on their back. Anyone who tried to go near them, without giving a second thought, they used to beat them up, they used to beat the people in the camp with their heavy boots till the prisoner turned into a lifeless pulp or was nearly dead.

In the room I was placed into, another family had already been living there for the past few months. There were two women, a man, and three kids who barely talked to one another. In the beginning, they were strangers to me, but then slowly I made friends with a girl who was a few years older than me. Her name was Selena and she was extremely beautiful just like a goddess who descended to the earth from the moon. She belonged to a Roma gypsy family, her features were a perfect combination of Indian and European blood. Her violet-colored eyes spoke volumes without uttering a word. Just like the rest, her eyes also concealed fear and grief, like my eyes or the eyes of everyone around. I feel the color of fear and grief is darker than violet or blue and this is the main reason why her eyes looked so colorless. She spoke the Roma language and I could understand some of it because Aunt Rebecca was from a Roma family and both Aidan and Jacob spoke Polish and Roma languages. I could speak a few sentences. One day, I spoke with Selena in her language, I asked, "Sarto ke jal?" (How are you?)

74

She turned around shocked.

"Fine azmangey," (I am fine) "Paari keraaf!" (Thank you)

Signaling to her family, I said, "Tonepo?" (Your family?)

Her reply in affirmation was very soft. Then, after some time, she thought about me and before she could utter the term "Tonpo" I shrugged my shoulders. Maybe, she understood because after that she never asked me about my family again.

Initially, for hours the two of us used to crouch in the corner and draw various pictures and lines on the floor, this was our idea of playing games. We invented various such games while sitting inside that room and they helped us pass the time, but soon everything came to an end when one day Nazi soldiers barged inside the building and signaled all the women and young girls to stand aside and leave the place in a queue.

My spine turned stiff with fear and premonition. The women in my room tried to hide Selena and other small girls behind them, but they were roughly dragged out and made to stand against the wall. I too had to stand in the row like the rest. Then, leaving behind small girls, all the women and young girls were pushed out of the room and led to the back of the camp. There was a field where on a railroad wooden dump carts filled with stones attached to iron rods stood. These dump carts were trains without engines. On its front, it had huge iron rods on both sides where thick ropes were tied. These ropes were tied around the women and girls who were then made to pull the dump carts. The wooden carts were filled with stones that weren't easy to pull and, in no time, women began to pant and sweat profusely. If the Germans wanted to, they would have got horses to do this task, but they didn't do it intentionally.

They were of the opinion that those in the labor camp must do heavy work even if it resulted in death.

"And then one day something strange happened." Zosia kept the page in her hand back inside her diary. Looking at me she uttered something in the Polish language.

Zobozu dobiegaly glosne krzyki

Startled, I looked at her because I could not understand a word she said.

Demony zaczely przesuwac pokrywy kominów przymocowanych do dachuobozu

The look on my face made her realize that she had gone back in time and was so lost that she began to converse in Polish. At that time, Zosia somehow collected herself and took a deep breath; holding back her tears, she managed to say,

"Zobozu dobiegaly glosne krzyki demony zaczely przesuwac pokrywy kominów przymocowanych do dachuobozu"

This means "And then heart-wrenching cries were heard from the camps because those evil men had finally begun to remove the lid from the chimneys on the terrace." Zosia repeated the sentence in Polish.

"That day, when they were pulling the dump cart train with ropes, that very afternoon Selena's parents and siblings were sent to the gas chamber and then their dead bodies were dumped in the truck like garbage. I saw Selena lying unconscious in the field and the sight made me vomit my guts out."

"Do you have the strength to listen to more?" Zosia looked at me with tearful eyes.

"No." I took a deep breath and then held Zosia's hands in mine; pressing them gently I said, "Come on, let's go home."

On our way back from the restaurant, both of us remained silent; I had no strength or power to say or ask anything, nor did Zosia possess enough words to voice anything. After a while, when I parked the car in front of her house, I saw her neighbor Tahseen Jaffri was parking his car in the garage; the moment he saw Zosia and me in the rearview mirror he recognized us immediately and, pulling down the side glass, he waved at us.

I waved back at him and then parked my car in front of Zosia's house, and then, climbing out of the car, I went towards her side of the car and opened the door for her. After saying thanks to me Zosia said, "Come inside, I will make a nice cup of coffee for you."

I didn't find it feasible to leave her all alone in the midst of nightmares; hence I accepted her offer and went inside the apartment following Zosia.

CHAPTER 9

When I woke up the next morning, I had a slight headache, but it was not possible to skip the office. A couple of files were pending, I had to complete those, and then I had to go shopping as well. For a long time, I had been avoiding certain stuff, but now it had become unavoidable, it was important to get all these errands sorted. Many times, after working in the office I felt exhausted and had no strength to buy groceries. Moreover, after five or six, the market often became crowded, every now and then there was something or other going on in the road. I had the information that today, in front of the Press Club, there was to be a protest march against the Indian army's oppression of the innocent Kashmiris in India. However, I was well aware of the fact that if I had to postpone my grocery shopping till such a time as there were no upheavals in the city then for sure my grocery shopping would remain due forever.

Hence, instead of waiting for the perfect day, I was to get my job done in any possible manner. The office was no relief; there too the entire day was spent editing political articles. On my return, when my car passed through the Press Club, the whole area was flooded by placards carrying images of youth and children. Either blood oozed from their eyes or they were submerged in teargas and smoke lying on the road in great pain. Unintentionally, and much against my will, I parked my car for some time and, pulling down the side mirror, I silently observed all those who had participated in the rally wearing red bandanas around their foreheads and carrying placards. The condition of the traffic was such that four rows of vehicles were connected to one another bumper to bumper and were literally crawling, horns blaring uselessly, and then the faces craning out of the cars' windows along with the hands making the victory sign and waving in the air, all these were making the environment take on a different form. Instead of a protest march that was supposed to mourn, it looked more like a carnival with a sea of people and a fleet of cars.

I was slightly aware of the political tussle between India and Pakistan over the Kashmir issue and I was more than confident that all these rallies and protest marches were nothing more than an easy route to reach the news headlines. The sole purpose of all these emotional extravaganzas is entirely different from what it appears to be, it is either the ruling party or the opposition that squeezes out maximum profit from them; never ever do these rallies and protest marches provide any solution to the actual problem.

After some time, I lifted up the window of the driving seat and, putting the car in reverse gear, I once again pulled out into the open road, slowly and gradually I tried to get out of the rush. As I was trying to pull out of the huge traffic jam, my eyes fell on a placard carried by a young girl who held it in both hands and raised it high above her head. Her placard read, "Oppression of the Indian army on the Kashmiri Muslims. Why is the world silent?" I stared at her placard for some time and then I felt the girl resembled Zosia's friend Selena and her placard read, "Oppression of the Nazi army on the Jews. Why is the world silent?" This sudden transformation made me realize the world is silent because for the past 75 years the world has still been standing where it once was, and when time stands still, the tongue is tied behind the cages of the lips and the voice that escapes these cages, instead of carrying meaningful messages, sounds like senseless rhetoric, something that has no solution or impact.

The previous night, while listening to Zosia's diary, I had thought of interrupting and asking her, "During those torturous moments, did you ever feel like cursing those devils who had destroyed your life, those who had pulverized your whole families, those who threw your parents into the gas chambers, shot them with bullets, killed them…. Did your eyes, while shedding tears of blood, ever look up into the sky and beg for wrath to be sent down upon these cannibals?" But I didn't ask her because I personally wanted to see if it was necessary for nature to do justice by bringing down wrath. And if this is true then there is no need to seek anything from such an insensitive nature, neither prayers nor curses.

———————— ◆ ————————

By the time I reached home, it was past six thirty and I had a pulsating headache. I took two tabs of paracetamol with tea and then lay down on the bed for some time. The moment I closed my eyes the rally in front of the Press Club began to raise slogans in front of my eyes, but now the face of the girl was replaced by the face of my mother. Blood flowed from Ammi's eyes and her face looked ashen with fear. She was crying profusely; Zosia was in her arms, but when I went near her, I came to know it was not Zosia but me. I clung close to her chest and she was crying, screaming, cursing loudly and looking at the sky. The faces in the cars were drenched in tears and they were carrying black flags in their hands, each one of them tailed the other silently in a mourning march. There was no sound of blaring horns or any noise of slogans; an ominous silence

80

prevailed everywhere, which was seared by the loud wailings and lamentations of my mother.

I woke up with a jolt. "Oh God!" I uttered. "What a scary nightmare." I formed fists with both my hands and started breathing deeply to relax.

Ammi came in my dreams after such a long time, but how? Dressed as those people!

All this is because of those political columns, congregations and rallies, plus the aftereffect of Zosia's life story. Everything looks the same to me now, I thought, lying there. *Gosh! How easily I get trapped by such thoughts and then begin to perceive the whole world in a single dimension. Come on, how can my poor old mother, the female protestor gathered outside the Press Club and Selene be interconnected? Oh, God!*

So many thoughts took shapes and forms of the images and faces inside my head and replaced one another and then everything culminated as a dream in front of me. But then all of a sudden an idea struck me and while lying down I removed the cover from my feet and sat up on the bed. I started to think.

My hands went to the drawer in the bedside table; I opened it a little and took out the black envelope from within. Once again I looked closely at the picture inside it where a white woman stood with a kid and at the back of the image "Zosia Casnova" and "Peter" were inscribed. Unfortunately, I didn't know either of the two languages, but I turned on the laptop and then on a piece of paper I began to write the Polish words in such a manner that they formed into sentences.

Piotr,

kiedy wrócisz do domu?

Czy nie wiesz, ze bolesne jest dla mnie pójscie na wojne ten sposób? Dlaczego we Wschodnim Pakistanie odbywa sie tyle dni? mam nadzieje, ze nie zlamiesz mi serca Odpowiedz na mój list lub mimo wszystko zadzwon do mnie

Mama
6 pazdziernika 1971

And then I started looking for their pronunciation in the Polish language, which came out of my mouth with great difficulty and in a weird manner, but as I began to decipher their meanings in Urdu, line after line, I realized that all these crooked characters were actually a letter.

Peter,

When will you return home? Don't you know it is a tad painful for me to see you go off to a war like this? Why is it taking you so long in East Bengal? I hope you won't break my heart. Make sure you reply to my letter or contact me on the phone.

Mom
16th October 1971

Then I opened another letter. It had just a few lines, but this one was written six months prior to the previous one because it was dated 25th Marca 1971, in the Polish language Marca means March.

Piotr,

Czy to prawda, ze ??zostales dodany do operacji Searchlight? Czy dolaczysz do skrzydla armii zmierzajacego do Pakistanu

Wschodniego? Co sie dzieje Dolaczyles do armii pakistanskiej bez mojej zgody, a teraz dolaczasz do tej strasznej wojny. Czy zdajesz sobie sprawe, ze nie moge bez Ciebie zyc? Chcesz byc z dala od swojej matki Nie wiem, dlaczego jestes taki zmuszony. Mozesz zostawic wszystko dla mnie i wrócic do domu Nie zapominaj, nienawidze wojny, która odebrala nam wszystko. Nasze zycie i nasz pokój.

Mama
25 Marca 1971

Peter,

Is this news true that you have been appointed to take part in Operation Searchlight? You are a part of the army wing going to East Pakistan? You joined the Pakistan army without my permission and now you are going to participate in this horrible war. Aren't you aware of the fact that I can't live without you? Do you want to stay away from your mother? I don't know what your concern is. Can you leave everything and come home for me? Don't forget I hate war; it is what snatched away everything from us … our lives, our peace.

Mama
25, Marca 1971

Hmm! So these are the letters Zosia wrote to her son, Peter, who participated in the 1971 war and went to East Pakistan from West Pakistan and Zosia was not happy about it and wanted him to come back to her. Everything is fine, but why are these letters and pictures with my mother? How did Ammi know Peter? What was the relationship between the two? Why did Ammi hide these letters and pictures inside the diary? Is it possible that Ammi came to Pakistan looking for Peter? What exactly is going on?

The train of my thoughts ran rampantly inside my head, but I realized I didn't have the answer to a single question.

Lord! I was back to square one. My situation was still the same, just like it was when I first found the black envelope in her diary.

I felt dejected.

What if I were to ask Zosia? Maybe she would know about everything?

No sooner did this thought enter my head than a few other thoughts rejected it instantly.

But I have already lied to her that I am a part of some NGO and our task is to survey the Europeans living in Karachi. This way I will lose all her trust and she won't tell me anything more about her life. I should continue digging intoher life story in the same manner till such a time as I get to know about Peter and his connection with my mother.

I continued to speak with myself in this way for a brief period and then placed the black envelope back into the drawer.

CHAPTER 10

Initially, I thought someone was banging on my neighbor's apartment door, but soon I realized it was my main gate that was creating such a dreadful noise. Someone was constantly banging at my door and continuously pressing the bell. The sound of the bell after each bang created a pulsating tremor inside my head. Frustrated, I rose from the bed and went towards the door; when I looked outside through the pinhole, my surprise knew no bounds, not only was Atya there but she was accompanied by Lubna and Shaista as well. These were my closest friends since my university days. All my frustrations evaporated in one single go and I jerked open the door, blinking my eyes in surprise and great happiness.

I said, "What is this? Am I dreaming or what?"

The three of them entered my apartment gaily, Lubna gave me a bear hug and Shaista smiled at me.

"Yeah, yeah, consider it a dream; now see for yourself we are invading your dreams as well."

Atya screamed as she barged in and sat on my bed like a child.

"When did you return from the U.S., Lubna? We had no news or information." I was hugged by Shaista when Lubna moved away.

"And you, Shaista, where the hell have you been, dude? Last I heard you shifted to Kuala Lampur after your marriage." After Lubna, it was time for Shaista's interrogation.

"God! I can't believe it." Once again I blinked and looked at the three of them.

"Looks like some early morning miracle."

"The sun rose from the west." Atya, Shaista, and Lubna cut me in the middle of my sentence chorusing unanimously. This made us all burst into laughter. Shaista and Lubna sat next to Atya on my bed and reveled in my bewilderment.

I pulled the sofa near to my bed and sat on it with my feet up and began to stare at them.

"Tell me now, how come all this has happened all of a sudden?" I asked them, looking at my wristwatch. "And it's seven in the morning."

"Nothing ya, just three days back Lubna came down from America and Shaista from Malaysia, and these two eminent personalities, out of their busy schedule, can allot just today to the two of us. So, I decided it was best to drag them here early in the morning without wasting a second before Her Highness leaves for the office and we scamper around half the day seeking her attention."

Atya chalked out the entire plan in one single breath.

"Now, it is for your good only that you call your office right away and give them some lame excuse about ill health. Get ready and let's burn down the city."

"That's great!" I agreed happily. "You did the best thing. Honestly speaking, Atya has become very sensible post-marriage." This made both Lubna and Shaista laugh their guts out.

"Yeah, yeah, it's all because of Dr. Sahab's company," Atya agreed flamboyantly and made us laugh at her expense. "The world stands witness to my wisdom before marriage," she added.

"Alight, okay, stop now. Lubna, how is everything between you and Ali Bhai?" I asked her.

"Everything is fine. Ali is good and so is Uzair," Shaista said, adding her husband's name.

"We could discuss all this all day; right now, you get ready and start moving so that we can leave as soon as possible."

"Alright," I replied. "Let me call my office first else there will be a huge ruckus there."

"Ahan! Madam hoity-toity is a hotshot journalist now, her absence will stall the entire press." Lubna attacked me in her typical friendly manner.

"Hush." Placing my fingers on my lips I gestured for them to remain silent as I called the office.

"Yes, Ghani Sir, please tell Rauf Sir I won't be able to come today, I am not feeling too well."

Atya, Lubna and Shaista glared at me with a naughty smile and no sooner had I hung up than they cried, "Allah o Akbar! You are such a big liar, Fatma! You are all hale and hearty, bloody lazy bones. '*I won't be able to come today; I am not feeling too well.*'"

The three of them were just impossible.

"Alright, okay, no more acting smart." I rolled my eyes animatedly and pointed towards the kitchen. "The hoity-toity hotshot journalist is going to get ready now; in the meantime, if any of you need anything, the kitchen is right there."

"No need, we will do breakfast, lunch, and shopping outside. You just go and get ready," Atya said, looking at Shaista and Lubna.

"Yes, yes, you just need to get ready fast, don't worry about us," Shaista added.

In no time, the four of us were leaving the building compound in Atya's car. I was feeling very happy at such a beautiful morning; thank God, I also got a break and got some time to unwind after being caught in the vicious cycle of a set routine for a long time. Definitely, Atya did me a great favor by uniting me with Shaista and Lubna. Once again, I felt like a young university student, someone who was free of all worries and spent hours talking to friends about nothing.

During my university days, we had a group of four girls who always stayed together. From bachelor's to master's degree, we were friends for four consecutive years. We belonged to different departments; for example, I was in the journalism department, Shaista and Atya belonged to the psychology department and Lubna was pursuing a master's in English literature, but it was impossible for us to stay apart before and after our lectures and we would talk about everything under the sun. Atya and Shaista got engaged during their bachelor's. Atya had got her Doctor Sahab and Shaista was happy with her fiancé, Uzair, who was pursuing civil engineering. During the final semesters of the master's degree, suddenly Lubna's hand was sought by Ali's family for marriage. Ali was an economist and was working as an executive in a multinational company based in Boston. Lubna and Ali got married in a jiffy and Lubna left for the U.S. without completing her master's degree.

My situation was always different; firstly, I was never too keen on the entire arranged marriage concept, and most importantly, from the moment I stepped into the university I fell helplessly in love with Asad. It wasn't just me; Asad too was crazy about me, he was less interested in his studies and was more occupied by me. Lubna and Atya always teased him by saying, "Looks like Asad Bhai attends university to do a Ph.D. in Fatma." Though he was pursuing a master's in English literature, all the romantic novels and poems derived their reference from his love life. Actually, we were not four but five friends, but Asad and I were a single entity with two different names. Shaista, Atya, and Lubna agreed with this fact from day one that Fatma and Asad were made for each other.

Our university days were a perfect combination of carelessness, friendship, and love, and instead of dreams of the future, they contained interesting gossip about the spicy present, but as soon as the master's degree came to an end, one after another, my friends left to pursue their own goals. First and foremost, Lubna left with Ali Bhai for America overnight, and then, in no time, Atya and Shaista also got married. Fortunately, Atya stayed in Karachi even after her marriage but Shaista left with Uzair Bhai for Kuala Lampur six months after they married. I was the only one left; well, after Ammi's death I had nowhere to go, it's a good thing I got a job as a journalist and also accommodation and I too got settled in life. I wanted Asad and I to get married, but Asad's male ego came in between that plan because it was impossible to get a job in Karachi with a master's in literature and he was adamant about remaining single until he could land a suitable job. Now, suddenly, he had got a job, but that was in ISI, I was baffled as to what someone with a literature background could do in ISI. But then I thought, *Maybe this will help us get ahead in life, we will be married soon, and jobs can change anytime.*

Suddenly, Shaista shook me vehemently. I found myself back in the present.

"Come on ya, I was lost in the university days, those were the days." I smiled.

"Yeah man, do you remember we used to have so much fun?" Just like me Shaista too found herself teleported to the good old university days.

"I feel student days are the best days of one's life," Lubna stated from the front seat.

"Especially college and university days because during those days one is slightly mature and knows what exactly is going on," Atya said, completing Lubna's sentence.

"Okay, listen now; let's drive to some nice restaurant for breakfast. I can't start my day without tea or coffee," I told Atya.

"Yes, of course, I know it." Atya slowed down a little at the red signal in Nursery.

"By the way, Your Highness, you are been taken to Marco Polo, we will be there in ten minutes," Atya notified all of us as she stopped the car at the red signal.

"The one at Club Road, in Pearl Continental?" Since I had dined there a couple of times I knew where she was taking us.

---◆---

The four of us found ourselves seated at a table at Marco Polo enjoying our breakfast. We were on a roll and talked endlessly, there was no end to our stories. First, Lubna narrated stories of America and how the two of them cherished each other from the day of their marriage till now. She was very happy with Ali. Similarly, Shaista could not stop gushing over her husband, Uzair. Verily, all three of my friends were very happy and content with their lives. In fact, I felt a flicker of doubt rise within me every now and then, but I did not allow it to take a bigger form. I submerged myself in the lives of my best friends so intensely that soon all my restlessness and suspicions were replaced by their happiness and joy.

After leaving Marco Polo, we moved towards Dalmon mall in Clifton and from there we came to Port Grind, where I shopped to my heart's content with my friends, and then, as per the schedule, we reached Do Darya where Doctor Sahab had already booked a table for us on Atya's insistence. Post dinner, as we relished our tea and talked about various stuff, suddenly Lubna asked me, "Fatma, we have shared all our stories and talked to our heart's content, but, man, what are your plans with Asad?"

Startled, I looked at her and asked, "What do you mean by plans?"

"Well, I mean how long are you going to wait for him like this? I mean there is a limit to everything. Come on, see for yourself, it's been two years since we finished our master's degrees, almost all of our friends are married."

"Yeah, you are right." I nodded and pretended to agree with her. "But, sweetheart, how do you set limits on love? And never ever have I thought of anyone else except Asad. Asad too is right there where he stood on the first day of our relationship. The truth, both of us are just as much in love with each other as we were back then, maybe our love has even intensified over the years," I replied, sipping tea.

"I understand everything, but marriage makes everything more practical because no matter how beautiful love and romance might sound, the fact remains if love is an architect's sketch then marriage is the building."

Lubna tried to impose her practicality upon me.

"Do you think a house is possible without a sketch?" I said playfully.

"Stop it now, Lubna." Atya interrupted us. "The relationship between Asad and Fatma is much more complicated and deeper than this. I know for sure Asad can't live without Fatma, neither it is possible for Fatma to live without Asad, their love is both romantic and platonic. Honestly speaking, I feel Fatma is extremely lucky she has someone who loves her so passionately and Asad is equally lucky to have a girl like Fatma who has dedicated her life solely to him. A love like this is rare in today's practical world."

I gave Atya a sideways glance from the rim of my cup and then, without saying anything, I took small sips from it. Shaista was silent

92

throughout the entire discussion; she listened to Atya, Lubna, and me with a smile on her face.

That evening, when I reached home, I felt fresh and rejuvenated. The whole day organized by Atya turned out to be a super hit. The way she stormed my apartment early that morning, she departed with the same noise along with Shaista and Lubna.

Standing in front of my dressing table, I stared at my reflection in the mirror for a long time and then, instead of hitting the bed, I sat with my laptop against the reading table. It was nearly 10:00 p.m.; the hands of the clock continued to rotate in the same manner as I rotated around Asad at all times of the day and night, and soon I escaped the confines of the clock and entered the realm of my heart and tried looking for ways to enter the heart of Asad.

Soon, my fingers danced on the laptop keys out of their own free will. In no time, I emailed the condition of my miserable heart through the medium of Tagore's poem.

Asad,

My beloved are you
Why do you stand behind everyone?
Concealing yourself in the shadow
Dust ridden and dirty path
People keep pushing you behind
They rush past you
Worrying you without any rules
I am here
From past so many hours
Standing still as I wait
Holding in my hands

Your gifts
All the passersby
Picking flowers one after another
Taking great joy
And my bouquet
Is getting emptied

The morning passed by
The noon also set
In the evening shade, sleepily
My eyes are getting heavy indeed
All those returning home
Look at me and smile
Embarrassing me to the core
And I
Like some begging girl
Pull a cloth against my face
Whenever they ask
What is it do I seek
I cast down my eyes
How am I to reply?
What is it that I say?

Verily, how can I tell them
I am waiting for your arrival?
Embarrassed, how can I say
You promised me you will come?
And I hold close this poverty
Like a dowry
Alas! This pride
Concealing in the deepest layers of my heart
I am waiting for you

And sitting here on the grass
Gazing at the sky without blinking
Waiting for your arrival
Dreaming about it
Everywhere there is a bright light
Golden flags sway on your chariot
The people on the road stare
You come down from your mighty chair
Proudly
So that you can lift me
And the beggar girl wrapped in rags
Hold her close to your bosom
Shy and proud
I shiver and shake
Like a swaying tree
In front of the stormy fall

But the time is flying by
The sound of your chariot wheels
Is still unheard
So many tableaus
Blowing their own trumpets
Went right past me
Is it just you
Behind all this
Under same shade
Standing all alone?
Is it just me
Crying her eyes out
Waiting for you
Carrying the wish to meet you in my heart
Concealing a futile desire of mine?

Yours
Fatma

CHAPTER 11

If it is ill health then it should last for two days at least, so what's the rush in getting well so soon?

This thought made me intentionally avoid calling the office the next day because I wanted the previous day's excuse, or rather lie, to appear real. I lay still on the bed for a long, long time and continued to think about Asad. When I closed my eyes, all the events of the previous day flashed through my eyes, the moment when Lubna asked how long I was going to wait for Asad like this. And at that time, I was searching for the proper words to explain, how I could've told her that, for me, time stopped the day he entered my life. For a long time, the hour and minute hands of the clock had turned into cupid's arrow for me and him. These arrows had replaced my heart with a wounded coffin of love. I was not even in a situation to express my condition to Asad, which is why I borrowed words from my beloved poet Tagore and sent them to Asad because I know for sure his intense expressions and my deep emotions would not go astray.

Oblivious to the mortal world, I swam and swayed into the river of love and land of romance. Suddenly, the mobile on my bedside table shrilled and brought me back to my room. Still lying down, I stretched out my hands and took the phone, it was Zosia calling. "Hello," I said.

"How are you, Fatma?"

"I am fine, thank you. How about you, ma'am?" I enquired, sitting upright on the bed.

"I am okay. We didn't speak yesterday, I kept thinking about you throughout the day. Many times, I thought of calling you but then refrained myself from doing so thinking you must be busy with work." Zosia continued to speak in the same soft voice.

"No, nothing of the sort. Actually, yesterday my university friends came to meet me out of the blue and together we celebrated our good old student life. I spent the whole day shopping and frolicking with them." I narrated the beautiful day to Zosia.

"Very well done, you did the best thing, old friends are like old wine, ever so intoxicating and inebriating. We can never have enough of them and they taste equally good every time we come in contact with them. There is a saying in Polish, *Nie dla wszystkich skrzypce graja,* which means violins cannot be played for everyone.

"True friendship is for a few only; always treasure your precious jewels, there is nothing more valuable than them." Zosya made my morning all the more beautiful with her beautiful way of talking.

"So, are you leaving for the office now or are you in the office already?" Zosia asked.

"No, I don't wish to go to the office today, I am going to stay at home instead," I replied.

"In that case, you come down here; I will treat you to Polish golabki rolls if you are interested in enjoying a different sort of lunch today. I don't know how interested you are in trying new varieties of cuisine." I accepted her offer instantly because, being a foodie, I loved enjoying new cuisine. Once in a while, Asad and I used to develop this craving to go and try new cuisines and search for Italian, Mexican, and Turkish restaurants. However, such restaurants were really scarce and the price was exorbitant, they were located in the posh areas of the city.

After I disconnected the call, my remaining tiredness evaporated and I tried to prepare myself mentally to head to Zosia's house.

———————◆———————

On reaching Zosia's home, she took me straightaway to her kitchen. I could see she was wearing a cooking apron and the fragrance of tomatoes, onion, and mushrooms wafted from her hands and kitchen. To date, I had never seen Zosia so happy and relaxed. At that moment, she did not look anything like a seventy-five-year-old woman; in fact, she looked ten years younger than her actual age. The way in which she ran around the kitchen was commendable. On one side of the gas stove, cabbage was getting boiled and on the other burner she sautéed finely chopped onions, mushrooms, and garlic with olive oil in a pan. I could see that she stopped every now and then and placed fine mince, tomato paste, rice, coriander, salt, black pepper, chili, etc. into a clean bowl and mixed it well. Zosia cooked like a professional chef and I could not stay silent for long; I finally asked, "Zosia, did you ever work as a chef?"

"For decades I have done loads of different work to survive, things I wanted to do and too many things I should not have done, but

99

sometimes we are not so fortunate as to get to do only the things we want to do, but, yes, cooking was one of the many types of work I enjoyed doing," Zosia replied without looking at me and then she tossed the veggies from the pan into the plastic bowl and began to mix them with the mince paste. Then she plucked the leaves of the boiled cabbage and placed them on a tray, and placing a spoonful of mince paste from the ball onto the cabbage leaves, she began to roll them. Within a few minutes, the tray was filled with more than a dozen golabki rolls ready to go inside the oven.

"Alright, now this will be ready in an hour and a half and I hope you will feel its taste in your mouth for years to come."

Placing the tray in the oven, Zosia fixed the temperature to 360 degrees.

"Come, while this thing gets ready, why don't you and I relax in the armchair in the backyard? I wish you to tell me something about yourself today, only if you wish to share something about your life with me."

"There is nothing worth sharing in my life, Zosia, everything is very plain and simple." With a soft smile on my face I followed Zosia out of the kitchen; we crossed a narrow corridor and went to the backyard. I saw the small home of Zosia was limited to a living room, bedroom, and kitchen. On the other side was a small wardrobe and restroom. There in the corridor, just next to the backyard, next to the door, stood a vintage European kind of washing machine on top of which a dryer machine was placed. Clothes and bed sheets were neatly stacked in boxes. Zosia's house was a reflection of her state of mind—well organized, calm, and composed. I felt life tried its best to pulverize and deform her, but in response to its attack, Zosia collected herself and decorated her life with equal ease and serenity. On the floor of the corridor, a Victorian-style carpet was spread, it had the same flowers that were present in the carpet of the living room, maybe this particular carpet was spread in different parts of the house at the same time. The walls of the corridor also had a few pictures here and there. These were pictures of Zosia and some other white people, the pictures were old and sepia in color but their frames were extremely beautiful and attractive, typical vintage-style photo frames. These pictures created a kind of sophistication in the corridor.

The moment I stepped into the backyard with her, I was spellbound. This part of the house too was a perfect example of Zosia's elegance. In one corner of the backyard vegetable plants were neatly potted, they were divided by sticks in such a remarkable manner; despite the small space it housed all the fresh vegetables one would need in one's kitchen—red and green tomatoes, lettuce, gourds, radishes, peas, turnips, beetroot, potatoes, carrots, coriander, mint, different types of chilies, spinach…. Zosia's garden literally grew everything one could imagine. There was a small grass corridor surrounded by a garden of various plants and it had a few cane garden chairs with a side and center table shaded by a colorful umbrella. The walls of the backyard and sides had big pots of roses, jasmine, and other fragrant flowers. This side of Zosia's house was extremely cool and peaceful, within a moment of my arrival my senses felt fresh and rejuvenated.

Silently, I looked around myself, but deep within I contemplated why up until now I was unaware I'd been leading my life in the manner I was. Why the hell was I so distant from nature? Day and night, leading a mechanical life, I was surrounded by machines only, and in this mechanical stream my real life was slipping away from me. I felt that a few days spent with Zosia were blessing me with a second life; on one hand, it led me through pitch-black nights and deep dark pits, and on the other hand, it elevated me to great heights and passed me through ebullient roads.

"My life doesn't have any such special event that's worth sharing with you, Zosia," I told her, sitting in a garden chair.

"All I ever had to call my own was my mother who succumbed to cancer a few years ago. In the year 1990, it was with her I settled in Karachi from Bangladesh. I was hardly two or three years old at that time. My mother was very poor, she did small jobs in people's houses and that's how we survived, but she had huge dreams for me, she wanted to give me a good education. Maybe that was one of the reasons why I continued to study and that's how two years ago I completed a master's in journalism from Karachi University, and now I work as a director and editor in an eminent news agency." I narrated my entire life story to her in a single breath.

"What about your marriage? Or are you still looking for your Mr. Right?" Zosia asked me with a gentle smile.

"Actually, I have loved Asad since my university days. We will marry soon, it's just that at the moment he is out of town due to his work." I told Zosia about my love life too.

"Good, you are a lucky girl and I hope and pray you always remain this lucky." Zosia's words made me smile.

"So, do you like my small backyard?" Zosia asked, looking around herself.

"Absolutely, I just love it and not only you are a great chef but an amazing gardener too." I complimented her one more time.

"True, many times trauma and stress result in sickness, it is at that time nature makes way for new treatments and cures," Zosia said very softly.

The two of us didn't know how the time passed as we discussed life and nature. Zosia excused herself to go to the kitchen. As she rose from her chair, I insisted vehemently that I would also tag along and help her with everything. The very thought that Zosia would cook for me and all I would do was eat was making me feel uncomfortable; moreover, it was useless for me to sit in the backyard all by myself. Once inside the kitchen, Zosia took out the tray from the oven and the pink rolls wafted an incredible aroma indicating they were nicely baked. The smoke coming from the rolls filled the entire kitchen with its gastronomical smell. Zosia placed the rolls delicately on the plates along with boiled, steamy unpeeled potatoes, carrots, cucumber, beetroot, and salad. She poured thick tomato sauce over the rolls and pushed forward the plate towards me.

"Let's go and sit at the dining table, the cutlery and soft drinks are already there. By the way, if you want you can warm these rolls and enjoy them with hot naan, these boiled potatoes taste awesome with hot naan."

I shook my hand in negation and said, "No thank you, I will eat it in the authentic style. I feel boiled potatoes, salad and rolls are an amazing combination."

Within a minute, the two of us filled the dining room with the soothing music of fork and knife. I decided that, after a heavy dinner of mutton roast, chicken, and biryani the previous night, this light healthy meal was nothing less than a blessing in disguise for my body. After lunch, I made green tea for Zosia and myself and the two of us carried our cups from the dining room to the living area and sat on the cozy couch. I silently anticipated listening to the remaining pages of Zosia's diary.

And then, in no time, without my wish escaping my lips it entered Zosia's heart silently and she lifted her diary. Turning to the folded page she started from where she had left off and, soon, we traveled to the harrowing horrors of her life seventy-five years ago.

$$\diamond$$

When Selena regained consciousness, she had lost all her senses. Crouched in the corner, she stared at the walls like a zombie. Whatever I said, my words fell back to me after hitting her lifeless form, but this was not the condition of Selena alone, everyone cooped up in those camps was an exact replica of her, they were nothing less than puppets devoid of all kinds of human emotions. Their eyes had dried and their bodies were soulless. Many men and women, just a shallow carcass, lay here and there on the camp floor waiting to be thrown into the gas chambers so that they could avail themselves of their share of huge graves and turn into fertilizer. As it is, their wait did not stretch longer than expected because each and every day a couple of them were sent to the gas chambers— inside that ominous chimney. Every day they were thrown into new graves.

My mind turned numb like the rest of the people in those camps, but somehow, I don't know why, I felt I was there to simply observe or rather witness everything; my fate was going to be different than the rest. I wish I had known my different fate was going to be more terrifying than theirs. Alas! I so wish I knew at that time that death at the hands of the suffocating gas chambers would have been preferable to the death my soul was going to be subjected to each and every day in the open atmosphere where I would be ripped off of all oxygen that let me breathe happily.

And then, one evening, when I saw the Nazi army defiling Selena's body like vultures, I was unintentionally reminded of my mother. I ran out of the hut and sat against a wall stuffing my head against a mound of cloth. I recited all the verses of the Torah under my breath, the verses Mama, Papa and I used to recite together. My tender heart shivered with pain, but the tears shed by my agonized heart drenched the walls of the camp. Maybe it was the time of the acceptance of prayers because the day after Selena died, the sky rained blood and the earth spat fire from everywhere. I could see the sky was covered with fighter jets, all the alleys and lanes were filled with the tunics of the Red Army and the sound of their armored vans reverberated everywhere. The camp walls shivered with the sounds of explosions every now and then. Smoke engulfed the city and nothing could be seen. On one side, Nazis abusing the Red Army threw grenades at them while in some places they opened fired at them, but soon as the Allied forces' attack intensified on the Nazis, not only did they retreat but they also ran through the streets to save their lives in exactly the same manner as the innocent Jews had run amok to save their lives only a few years ago. Chances are the patience of the Creator had reached its limits and the day of judgment had finally arrived. I don't know why I felt all this was because of my lamentations and prayers; perhaps it was because, on that particular night, I cried and recited this particular verse of the Torah over and over again:

Jestes moja kryjówka; uchronisz mnie od
klopotów i otoczysz piesniami wybawienia – Selah

Lord, you will shield me from these oppressors, protect me from the pain and wrap me with the verses of salvation – Selah

But to me, this truth appeared very different because in no time the scene outside on the road, explosions in the alleys and buildings, reached the camps too. The Nazis created fronts in the camp and began to open fire; the sound of grenades and bombs shook the camp walls and ceilings, and in no time, the roofs and chimneys began to fly up into the air, walls collapsed to the ground, people in the camps and Nazis tumbled over one another. Fire, smoke, rubble and cries and the poisonous state devoured everything in no time along with me—I don't know for how long.

———————◆———————

I opened my eyes in Bavaria. I have no idea when and how I reached Germany from Poland. All I remember is that I was taller than before, my hair was blonder and my body had transformed into a grown-up girl, but I was on the thinner side and there were dark circles under my eyes. I stood inside the room with the support of the wall and my hands played with the belt tied at the back of my dress. I was wearing long stockings and the strap of one of my shoes had come off, which was why I kept putting my toes in and out of the shoe. Johan stood right next to me; he was thin and had blue eyes just like mine, his hair was reddish brown and curly, maybe he was a year or two younger than me. There in front of the sofa sat a couple aged around fifty or sixty who looked like farmers and in front of them sat a young man wearing an army uniform who spoke with them in German. I guess he was a government official, maybe a welfare officer or a military man who was taking our information from the two of them. He thought maybe the two of us were not their real kids but stolen Polish foster kids who were settled here during the war with the sole purpose of Germanization. He also spoke with us from time to time and every time we replied, he confirmed the facts with our new parents.

"Wussten sie, wer ihre leiblichen Eltern waren?" the officer asked both of them. (Do you know who their biological parents are?)

"Sie sind tot," the woman replied. (They are dead.)

Startled, I looked at Johan, who was busy digging at the floor with the toe of his shoe.

"Woher wusste sie, dass die Eltern der Kinder tot waren?" the officer asked the woman, fixing her with a hard gaze. (How do you know their parents are dead?)

"Sie sagten uns," the woman replied in the same tone. (They say that.)

"Wer sind sie?" (Who are "they"?) The officer stressed the term THEY.

"Die anderen Leute," the woman muttered. (They are the other.)

"Thousands of people in Eastern Europe were searching for their lost kids."

Tausende osteuropäische Eltern suchten nach vermissten Kindern.

"East Europe – East Europe."

Osteuropa – Osteuropa.

The woman spat the word hatefully.

"Our kids have got nothing to do with the East; these kids are German orphans, look at their faces."

Unsere Kinder haben nichts mit "Osten" zu tun. Sie sind deutsche, deutsche Waisenkinder. Sie müssen sie nur ansehen.

This time her husband literally cried as he insisted.

"No need to get so emotional."

Keine Notwendigkeit, emotional zu sein.

I looked like the officer did not approve of the way her husband addressed her loudly; seeing this, the woman placed her hand on his.

"You people must be aware, just like in Poland, millions of children from Romania and Yugoslavia were brought here to fulfill General Greifelt's dream of Lenboren Society."

Sie wissen, wie Rumänien und Jugoslawien wurden Millionen von Kindern aus Polen hierher gebracht, um zu germanisieren, um den Traum der Lebensborn-Gesellschaft von General Greifelt zu erfüllen.

The officer did not stop just there; he proceeded to look at us affectionately and sighed.

"In the history of humanity, this is the worst example of genocide."

Ah, dies ist das schlimmste Beispiel für Völkermord in der Geschichte der Menschheit.

At this, the woman's husband once again tried to confirm his view.

"This is true these kids were found in the Eastern region, but they are German orphans, they explained it to us in clear terms."

Es ist wahr, aber diese Kinder wurden in den östlichen Gebieten gefunden, aber sie waren deutsche Waisenkinder. Das haben sie uns sehr deutlich gesagt.

"Are you happy here?"

Bist du glücklich hier?

This time the officer asked the question looking at the two of us.

We looked at our new parents and nodded in agreement.

"Do you go to school?"

Gehst du zur Schule

Once again, we looked at our new parents and nodded in agreement.

"Do you work in the fields?"

Arbeitest du auf dem Bauernhof?

"Only at times," Johan muttered softly.

Manchmal.

The officer looked at us one more time, and then at our new parents, and then collected different forms into a bundle; he stuffed them inside his black leather bag and, rising from his chair, he said, "I will once again trouble all of you to complete this procedure."

Ich kann Sie erneut stören, um diesen Prozess abzuschließen.

On the departure of the officer, the woman locked the door from inside and looked at the two of us; this time she told us in Polish, "You are ours and will remain ours. Now, go back to your rooms and get ready to sleep, don't forget you need to go to the fields as well."

Jestes nasz, bedziesz nasz. Teraz idz do swoich pokoi i przygotuj sie do lózka. Nie zapomnij o pracy w polu wczesnie rano.

This did not surprise me much, maybe the events of the last few months or years had escaped my memory or just become a daily affair, but every now and then something new also developed; so far, I had kept it to myself alone. This was a new feeling that often startled me from a deep sleep. The feeling was stirred by those hands that intruded beneath my blanket in the middle of the night and got busy touching different areas of my body. Sometimes, they traced the young roundness of my breasts and at other times they crawled into the area between my thighs. During sleep, when I jerked those hands away, they halted for some time but then again returned to tracing the top and bottom parts of my youth, and whenever I sat up with a start, they disappeared from my room nervously. Maybe this was something that was going on for days, which is why, like a routine, it resumed that night too.

In the night, when I woke up, I assumed maybe these were Johan's hands because his room was right next to mine, but that night I cried with agony when he mounted my frail body with his heavy weight. Before my scream could escape the room, he put his hands on my mouth with full force and, tearing off my clothes, left me all bleeding and bruised.

That time, I saw that person was not Johan but my new father—the farmer.

CHAPTER 12

That night, when I returned home from Zosia, my mind was benumbed. Each and every meeting with Zosia started off happily and always culminated in extreme tragedy and depression. After each meeting, my heart said that I must not listen to any more of the pages from her diary. In those pages, stories were hidden that belonged to her past, but every time they escaped the leaves of the pages, they pierced through my heart like arrows. They may have been dead stories of the distant past, but the moment they left that diary they took on the shape of a multi-faced snake that began to devour its own characters. I liked meeting Zosia because my soul felt at peace with her, but every time I returned home after meeting her, the very same soul was set on burning fire. Meetings with her caught me in between two extremes of happiness and grief and I wanted to get rid of this pain; I knew it was impossible to get rid of the pain without undergoing the whole ordeal, which was filled with the calamities and ordeals of Zosia's life.

It was best to shut out all thoughts from my mind for some time I thought and, changing into comfortable pajamas and a T-shirt, I sat in front of my laptop. When I checked my email, I saw a reply from Asad; it was in reply to the poem of Tagore—a delicate poem by him. Maybe he was able to feel the pangs of my longing and he too wanted to see the light of my love light up his life. The fact was both of us were gripped by the pain of loneliness and every second of life was engrossed in a deep longing for each other. I took a deep breath and soaked myself in the melody of his poem. I let it enter my heart through my eyes.

On the verge of a lonely empty river
Next to the swaying green grass
I had asked this
O beautiful!
Hiding the lamp under your cloak
Where are you going all alone?
My home is all dark and lonely
Give me all your light
Hence for a minute, she
Turned her kohled eyes up
And looking at me
She said hiding behind the evening
I have come to the river
When the bright day meets its dusk
And hides its face behind
I will hand it over to the waves
My lamp
Standing alone in the crowd of grass
Kept staring
The flickering lamp
In the waves
Kept swaying around

Hence, in the silence of the night
I had asked her one more time
O beautiful, this home of yours
Filled with light
Then why do you carry the lamp

Where are you off to?
Give me your light
Hence for a moment she
Turned up her kohled eyes
Looked at me suspiciously
Finally, she said
I am here because
I want to offer my lamp to the sky
Standing there, I kept staring at that lamp
Flickering uselessly in that lone space

On the latter half of a dark night
There was not a sliver of moonlight
I had asked her this
O beautiful, what do you seek
Holding this lamp so carefully?
Where are you going?
My home is dark without a soul
Give me your light
She stopped for a moment
Thinking something she stared into the dark
She said
I have brought the lamp
To make it a part of
A party of light
I stood there looking at her
Losing myself in the blinding light

The poem filled me with immense peace. I felt it worked on my restless heart that was pining for Asad in our separation and the depression caused by the painful stories of Zosia like an antidote. Sitting in the chair, I breathed softly with my eyes closed and let each and every word of the poem seep into every pore of my body.

After some time, when I opened my eyes, I looked at the subject of an email right after Asad's email. I clicked on it instantly. This email was from Bangladesh High Commission notifying me that my application for the visit visa had been approved and I was directed to submit my passport, photographs, and visa fees at the High Commission office. I felt this happened before time because I was expecting that email to arrive after a few weeks, plus I hadn't said anything about booking leave in my office.

When I checked my phone, there were multiple messages there, one of which was from Atya, and two texts were from Shaista. Shaista had sent a goodbye voicemail from the airport whereas Atya's texts were generic. One message was from Rauf, my boss, who asked me about my health and also made mention of the pending work that was piling high. I instantly called him and informed him that I intended to be back in the office the next day, which I am sure made him breathe a sigh of relief. After hanging up the phone, my eyes fell on the wall clock and I was taken aback by the time, it was just 6:00 p.m. now. I had no need to go to the kitchen and cook because, before I left Zosia's house, she packed around half a dozen golabki rolls along with boiled potatoes and salad and handed them to me. Suddenly, I thought of Atya and called her instantly.

"Listen, Atya, would you like to have golabki rolls?"

My out-of-the-blue question made her retaliate with, "What the hell is that?"

"It's a heavenly, extremely tasty dish you would love to taste."

I told her about the lunch at Zosia's and she asked me to come down to her instantly as she was the one who always tried to cook and taste new cuisines among the group of four. Moreover, I did not

114

want to get bored in the evening sitting all by myself at home. The depressing fog caused by Zosia's stories needed an antidote of the supercharged energetic talks of Atya. Hence, I picked up the food pack Zosia had given me, locked the door, and took out my car once again.

———————◆———————

On reaching Atya's home I saw a huge gathering in total swing. Stupid Atya didn't even tell me that her family and friends were invited over for dinner. Here I was standing in front of them casually clad in simple clothes, but the best part is everyone over there was talking to each other freely and with total frankness. In no time, I became a part of that dandy group; soon the discussion shifted to politics and everyone began to talk about the Kashmir issue. I thought all of them were concerned about the oppression in the Valley.

Suddenly one of the gentlemen said, "The across-the-border government is trying to Indianise our Kashmiri brothers from Kashmiri to Indians, they are trying to change the familiar majority and put their control over Kashmir."

This sent me back to the world of Zosia, maybe her painful and hard-hitting story was not to be so easily expiated by a poem of Tagore or the exciting get-together at Atya's. It seeped into the very core of my being and from there entered my soul, and a mere mood change was not something that would erase it from my life. In no time, I saw Kashmir getting transformed into the Ghetto of Warsaw and too many trains carrying Kashmiri women and children being transported to camps built specifically to put them into gas chambers. I shivered at that thought and returned to the dining table.

After some time, I excused myself and went out onto the balcony; standing there I stared at a flock of birds following one another. I saw that during the flight the big birds surrounded the small birds so that their children wouldn't lose their way and get separated from their families.

———————◆———————

That night, on returning home, my mind wandered off to the same world once again, the world where it was stuck before going to Atya's home. When I lay down in bed to sleep, there was no sign of sleep in my eyes and an innumerable amount of vagabond thoughts flooded my mind like a swarm of butterflies. Every thought was draped in a color of its own and every color asked questions about its existence. At times the questions turned so big that the whole universe would get inside them and at times they became so small that they were barely visible. Sometimes they turned into huge birds covering the whole sky with their wings and sometimes the small birds, their children, during the flight wailed loudly out of fear that they would lose their way. At times, not just their colors but their shapes changed too; sometimes they turned into Zosia and at times they turned into Ammi and flew around me or soared far away towards a distant horizon. Sometimes, they turned into the shape of Selena or Zosia's mama and begged the Nazi army to spare their honor or they took the shape of an inhuman farmer-father who defiled his foster daughter. They tried to enter the earth in the shape of a mother but then soon there rose within them Muslim, Hindu, and Jewish people; Jammu and Kashmir, Ladakh, Poland, Yugoslavia, and Romania erupted in the form of ghettos, which were attacked by tanks, flying jets, and explosives that pushed them inside the camps and opened the lids of gas chambers.

It was a train of never-ending torturous thoughts that ran non-stop crossing all stations carrying innumerable girls resembling Zosia and too many men of the Russian Red Army who carried them in different bogies as the bounty of war.

"But Zosia, they came to Europe to end the Nazi occupation in Germany, so how did all this happen?"

When I asked Zosia about it in the afternoon, at that time, instead of giving a reply to my question, she continued to read the next page of her diary.

"After the rape, when I opened my eyes in a nearby hospital in Bavaria, the social services representative there rehabilitated me in a shelter house temporarily. There were too many girls like me in that shelter house who were taken there following the rape or sexual abuse they endured at the hand of their foster fathers. But all of us had one major similarity, all of us belonged to East Europe, and the majority of them were Jewish and Gypsies who were kidnapped and Germanized so that their lineage could be turned into a better race."

Reading this Zosia gave a sarcastic smile. Looking at me she taunted, "We were a free crop, Fatma, anyone who got hold of us owned us. My story was one of a kind; my mother was brutalized by the Nazi attackers and I was assaulted by the protective Red Army. Never in my wildest dreams did I imagine that, hugging the Paszo camp wall, the prayers I called for crying profusely would lead to such dreadful events."

"What do you mean?" I asked her apprehensively; maybe I was losing the strength to know the truth further.

"I and a few other girls were captured by the Russian soldiers and were taken to their army camp. I was only fifteen or sixteen at that

117

time and there were dozens of soldiers there. They divided the girls among them and at times they took us alone or in groups. After several weeks, when they were finally done, they threw me in the brothels of Berlin. Within a few years, I turned into a dark figure of those dark alleys whose face was so distorted that I could not recognize who I was looking at in the mirror."

Zosia inhaled deeply and looked at me and then stared out the window for a long time.

"I was not alive during that period; I was a dead soul. Those pages of my life are totally blank, I have nothing to tell you except that one day I got pregnant by some unknown man, and instead of aborting the child, I decided to leave Europe forever.

CHAPTER 13

The next day in the office was extremely busy. Rauf Sahab was right; within a span of two days too many columns had accumulated for editing. My fingers danced on the keyboard swiftly and the paragraphs of different columns passed through my eyes like a long train. I was trying my best not only to finish a good part of two days' pending work but also, if possible, to send my passport, photograph, and other documents to the office of the Bangladesh High Commission for a visa through the DHL courier of Islamabad. For a minute I wondered, *What if Rauf Sahab poses a hindrance to my week-long leave for the Bangladesh trip?* Hence I also tried to complete some of the work in advance. In no time it turned into a very busy day and I postponed sending off the visa parcel until the next day. While leaving the office, my mind wandered off to Zosia and I thought why not meet her on my way home, but then I told myself we'd met just the day before and it wouldn't look good to drop in at her house without warning. Western people are very particular about all that.

On reaching the parking lot, before starting the car, I could see Rauf Sahab come out of his vehicle and when he saw me, he began to wave at me. I thought he was calling me or trying to say something, so instead of turning towards the main gate, I swerved my car towards him. He told me that next week he wouldn't be able to come to the office because for the TV channel he had to attend a meeting with PEMRA and would be going to Islamabad, which meant I would have to look after everything at the office. I thought, *Thank God, now I won't have any problems as far as leave for Bangladesh is concerned.* On hearing this I said, "No problem at all, I will take care of everything."

My reply made him relax instantly and he smiled. I felt as if I had taken a big burden off his shoulders. And I thought, *Why don't I take some work home as well? I don't have anything important to do today.* This made me stop at the parking lot and go back to the office. I collected a few papers from there and returned to my car. When I reached home, I realized that, even after a strenuous day, my mind was very relaxed, but when I sat down to work I realized the long day had tired me physically and it was not possible to work anymore.

I shut down my laptop and sat on the bed.
Closing my eyes, I began contemplating who I was.
What's my reality?
Where do I come from?
Where will I go?
Who are these people around me?
What is this place?
And then Zosia invaded my mind.

Just like me, she too was heading from one unknown to another unknown on an unknown quest. My heart began to sink from within. I felt my loneliness was my enemy; she always pushed me to unknown paths and compelled me to search for an unknown destination. I recalled when Zosia met me for the first time; she asked me, "What would you get by joining the broken pieces of history?"

And I replied very confidently, "COMPLETION." Now I was asking myself, *Is that so? Really?*

I felt deep inside myself confidence is getting replaced by restlessness. Chances were, after completing the entire story, I would become incomplete and remain incomplete forever.

What if a few missing pages of life after coming together turned the whole meaning of life meaningless?

Where would I go with this meaningless reality?

Without accidents, life is fogged by a shield of misunderstandings or false hopes, which at least makes it beautiful enough to make the journey easy and here I was in the midst of stifling accidents trying my best to create a path. I didn't know where this road would take me, whether it would sink me into a black pit or take me to bright heights.

And what if, after knowing the truth of life, I lost all interest in it?

What if the quest took me to a destination I was not searching for?

Surrounded by innumerable questions, I dozed off and I saw a stranger in my dream who told me from afar, "I am your father." I ran towards him, but within a fraction of a second, he vanished from sight. On waking up in the morning, even after trying like crazy, I could not recall the face of the father I saw in my dream.

The next few days were extremely busy because handling Rauf Sahab's responsibilities meant client contacts and meetings throughout the day, getting performance feedback from all the departments in the office, proper check and balance of business, and all this topped by my own work, my columns, editing of news and articles, etc. My schedule was so hectic that most of the time I reached home at eight or nine at night. Even then the work did not get completed because every night, on returning, I narrated the day's work to Rauf Sahab, took suggestions from him, also took the schedule for the next day, prepared a checklist, and completed a few pieces of editing at home. Finally, on reaching the weekend I took a sigh of relief, slept late into the morning, and when I left the bed at eleven, Zosia was the first person who came to my mind because throughout the week I didn't get a chance to speak with her once.

When Zosia replied to my call, the usual exuberance I was so used to was missing from her voice. She told me she had not been keeping well for the last few days and she was not in a mood to meet me. On Friday, the post contained my passport stamped with one month's Bangladesh visa. I thought, *Why not book a flight for the coming Monday?* My exhaustion would go and Rauf Sahab would easily sanction my leave. As it was, he was thrilled by my performance over the week, and also suggested indirectly that I must take some rest because two days after my illness I had worked a double shift for an entire week and did two people's work, it was necessary for me to take some rest. Before booking the ticket and searching for hotels online, I called up Rauf Sahab and asked him for a week off; even before I could complete my sentence he said, "Fatma, even if you didn't tell me this I would have requested you take some rest before you come back. I know how important you are to this office."

Not only was Rauf Sahab a good human being, but he was also well aware of his employees' flaws and skills. In the last two years, he added the title of editor and director before my name because he wanted to see me in the office forever. I availed myself of Monday's flight from PIA very easily because every week five flights left from PIA to Dhaka.

That evening, when I returned home after shopping, the first thing I did was write an email to Asad. Initially, I thought I would keep my mail very short and crisp, just let him know that I was leaving for Bangladesh, but, as usual, I couldn't do it; my fingers continued to dance on the keyboard and I bared open my heart and self to Asad by filling him up with one detail after another.

Asad,

For the past few days, I have been on a quest to know who I am, and in this quest, I don't know whether my search will actually introduce me to my real self or leave me in a nowhere land without any knowledge or trace of self or identity. I don't have any idea between the path and the destination which one is more important? I want to reach either the axis or the extreme of this adventurous journey; chances are, after this, both the road and the destination will lose their meaning, but then even that meaninglessness will give a new meaning to my life. Therefore, I feel this deal is not futile. The moment I read this poem by Parveen Shakir I realized the missing pieces of my puzzle are just like the lost leaves of my life that are hell-bent on coming together and forming one comprehensive whole. Chances are you too might have read it.

Strange is this issue of evolution that benumbs the brain
All the contradictions
To their predetermined nature
Accumulate from somewhere
Then, in total silence,
One day return to the predestined path
For eternity, the circle of life

Is constantly in a state of a voyage
The agreement of contradictions takes a uniform shape
In search of sustenance, the body might break down its fences
At times all the skills will melt down to the fist
At times the swords will get unsheathed
Garbage, slums, ghetto, and skyscrapers
Spread on the earth
At times slow and gradual
At times all of a sudden
And every now and then
In both situations
All we seek is our lineage
That exalted blood, those elevated tribes
It's there the family tree lies
Dense hair, presentable visage, health and high
Becomes all silent and rife
After that, there is just one destiny
One moment
One century
Vanishing from the eyes

But the truth is
If a little bit of fact is mixed into the sight
One day, an introspection of self
If only we can see,
Then this invisible group will come to light
All the missing pieces
Will come right to us
If we muster a little courage
And have the heart to look into the mirror when no one's there
Then maybe
We don't need to try so hard

Asad,

After Ammi's demise, I found in her diary a few pages and pictures of a white woman named Zosia and her son Peter. I don't know how come a poor, simple Bengali girl like Ammi would protect them with her life. Somehow, I managed to locate that white woman and her child, but till now I haven't been able to learn about her relationship with Ammi because in her story there is no mention of Ammi. I am going to Bangladesh to find out about the relationship because, in this quest, even if I can't find Ammi, still there is a great chance of unearthing a few missing pages of lost history. The truth is, now more than Ammi, Peter, and that Western woman's connection, I am keener than ever to know about their shattered life, which is lost somewhere in this long journey.

I am flying to Dhaka with PIA on Monday. During this time, I am going to stay at the Intercontinental Hotel in Dhaka.

Yours
Fatma

CHAPTER 14

The moment my flight landed at Shah Jalal International Airport in Dhaka I felt myself being gripped by magnetic powers from all sides. I was face-to-face with an inexpressible feeling, maybe because this place was my motherland, I was born here, or maybe because my mother saw many ups and downs here. On coming out of the airport, I found the atmosphere dense with humidity, either it was due to the Bay of Bengal or the effect of my mother's tears that pervaded the whole environment. On leaving the airport, when the taxi sped past Memon Singh Highway, the breeze from the Brahmaputra River began to melt down the ice around my heart. I could feel a sense of freshness within me, but then soon it began to diminish as the Dhaka traffic started to get on my nerves. Thank God, here the traffic was not as bad as in Karachi, mainly because on crossing the Banani overpass I could see the proud Intercontinental Hotel standing aloft in its white glory. On reaching it I realized that the airport, hotel, the roads, everything appeared very familiar to me because after leaving Karachi I had looked at all these places very keenly. A kind of relief engulfed me when I reached my hotel room because, in comparison to the rest of the hotel, the room was extremely impressive. On the departure of the porter, I called up room service and ordered food and placed my clothes in the wardrobe from my bag. It was 7:00 p.m. At that time, I told myself it was not sensible to leave the hotel at that time, plus I was to schedule my plans in such a manner that I could make the most of those five days there. I had to do all I could to unearth the connection between Peter and my mother and my task was to look for the right link to untangle this knot.

◆

The next day, on waking up, the first thing that came to my mind was I remembered I had found a few numbers in Ammi's diary. I decided to try those numbers hoping to get some leads from there, but then before calling up those numbers I got ready, changed my clothes and went down to the lounge. I went to the receptionist sitting at the desk, asked her about the breakfast and went to the café. The time was 7:30 in the morning but the café was more or less full, I picked up a plate and stood in the queue for the buffet. It was nice to see that everything was spick and span, the food was fresh and the service and ambiance impeccable; the waiters were swiftly working the tables. While I was busy having my breakfast at a table, a pleasant-looking girl arrived and excused herself, seeking permission to share the table with me. I looked around, seriously, the whole café was full. The girl was around my age only, more or less 24–25, she was wearing a beautiful red blouse paired with a thick embroidered silken cream-colored saree, her saree was embroidered with flowers in red thread. The way she had wrapped the saree around her petite figure with the ends thrown around her left shoulder made her look exquisite. She thanked me in a very soft voice saying, "DHANYOBAD."

When I said, "You're welcome," she gave me a sideways glance and then got busy spreading the jam on her toast.

Sipping her tea, she looked at me and asked, "Are you a Pakistani or Indian?"

I replied softly, "I am from Pakistan."

"I could tell from your clothing."

This time she chose to speak in English instead of Bengali.

"But I was born in Bangladesh."

I tried to break the ice. "It means genetically you are from Bangladesh and physically you are from Pakistan."

She laughed and nodded, looking at me. This made me laugh as well. "That's true."

Soon, she finished her breakfast and she said formally, "It was nice chatting with you," and rose from the table.

I said, "You talked a lot with me but didn't introduce yourself," to which she took out a visiting card from her purse, handed it to me, and left.

The visiting card read, "Kalpana Dutta, Director, Liberation War Museum." I gave the card a fleeting glance, put it inside my bag, and left the table.

Before going to my room, I stood at the reception desk for some time and asked, "Will you help me in finding the addresses of a few phone numbers?"

The receptionist gave me a heartwarming smile and said, "Why not?" I took out a chit from my bag where two names were written before the numbers—Shamshad Begam and Roshan Ara.

128

Unfortunately, Shamshad Begam's number did not exist anymore whereas Roshan Ara's number had changed and another one continued to ring without any response. The receptionist told me that in the last five years very many numbers had become obsolete; in fact, too many locations had their area code changed, but on my request, she saved those numbers and assured me that she would seek the information of those clients from Bangladesh Telecommunication Department and give me an update soon.

I had been in my room for less than thirty minutes when the phone rang; on the other end was the receptionist whom I had charged with finding out the details of the numbers. She told me there were no records available in the office for Shamshad Begam's number, hence nothing was known about Shamshad; however, the second number, belonging to Roshan Ara, was from Tangail, a district located within two hours' distance from the northwest side of Dhaka. She tried to explain the address to me, but I told her to write down the address on a piece of paper and, if possible, try calling Rosha Ara once more after some time, maybe somebody would answer from the other end. After four hours the reception told me that instead of Roshan Ara the number now belonged to Abdul Manan who was her relative and using her phone. He didn't tell her much about Roshan Ara, just talked about vague stuff and disconnected the call.

The fact is that the receptionist helped me more than I had expected. My biggest problem was the Bengali language because I was thinking if I went to Tangail and talked to Manan Sahab about Roshan Ara directly, chances are I would get some information from him and this way I would get to know the details about Ammi's past life in Bangladesh. It was 2:00 in the afternoon and Tangail was two hours way, which meant the drive to and from from Tangail would stretch till night as I had no idea how long it would take at Tangail. I thought of talking to that receptionist one more time asking her if she could arrange a ride from the hotel itself then all this could be done smoothly and in a much better way. I straight away went to the lounge to meet with the receptionist instead of calling from my room. Locking the room, I waited for the lift in the corridor.

◆

I spent the remainder of the day exploring Dhaka because the receptionist promised me that she would arrange for a cab the next day that would take me to Tangail and bring me back to the hotel, and the best part was that the driver could fluently speak English along with Bengali. I was visiting Dhaka for the first time because, naturally, I didn't remember a thing from when I was a toddler. Dhaka's lanes, roads, markets, parliament building, Shaheed Minar, Dhaka University, Dhakeshwari Temple, Lal Bagh Fort, and the tour of old Dhaka city made me feel like I was in Karachi or old Lahore. At times I felt proud looking at the clean roads of Dhaka whereas the filth and rush of certain areas made me feel suffocated, but along with these two extremes, the thing I loved best about Dhaka was the hospitality of the Bengalis, their friendly behavior and simplicity that gave me a sense of belonging. The day passed like a breeze.

That evening, on returning to my room, I was quite accustomed to the people of Dhaka. After freshening up, I ordered dinner in my room. As I was about to lie down on the bed, the phone in the room rang. I was taken aback by the voice on the other end, it was none other than Asad; he sounded restless.

"You went to Dhaka all of a sudden? You didn't even express any such plans in any of your previous emails, and now this … all of a sudden—"

"Hello, Asad." Hearing his voice filled me with insurmountable joy and I interrupted him in the middle of his sentence, "How are you?"

"Forget about me, tell me what is troubling you enough to drop a bomb on me out of nowhere and go to Dhaka and all alone too, you could have at least taken your friend Atya with you."

There was anxiety and shock in his voice, which was why, without thinking anything, he had called me straight away.

"Yes Asad, it was difficult to bring Atya along, she has her own responsibilities, plus all this is too personal and there is absolutely no use sharing all this with her," I replied to him.

"I know you are very confident and independent, but still, traveling all alone to an unknown country is making me worry a lot." Like always, Asad expressed his love keeping my feelings in mind.

"Asad, my visa came all of a sudden, and then the office arranged my leave for this week only, I had no idea when I would get an opportunity like this again." I explained the reason for this sudden trip to Bangladesh.

"Well, I know you will take care of yourself and will be successful in your endeavor," Asad said, trying to motivate me.

"Asad, I want to know one thing." Before Asad's call could end, I asked him the question that had been worrying me for quite some time.

He remained silent for a while; I guessed he was waiting for my question.

"When are you going to return?"

"Very soon. I know you are missing me terribly, but don't forget I am equally miserable without you."

"Asad, do keep in mind I will wait for you all my life." I poured my heart out to him and told him everything.

In reply, he just said, "I love you," and the call was disconnected.

Holding the receiver in hand, I stared blankly, and when there was no callback, I put back the receiver on the cradle.

CHAPTER 15

The next morning, I woke up early, hurried through my breakfast, and left for Tangail. The distance from Dhaka to Tangail was much less than I expected. I had assumed it to be two hours long, but it took us only an hour and fifteen minutes to reach there. One of the reasons might have been the time of day; at that time, there was heavier traffic in the opposite direction meaning the number of vehicles moving from Tangail to Dhaka was much more than the vehicles going to Tangail from Dhaka. Moreover, only sometime back a new highway was erected between the two cities where the traffic lights were nearly zero. The city, located on the banks of Loha Jung River, was so lush that it gave out a picturesque impression of being an establishment built over moss. There was a pleasant nip in the air paired with warm sunlight, which did not turn the weather harsh, but the women on the road clad in colorful cotton sarees carrying bright umbrellas appeared every now and then adding to the color of the place. In the area of the city in which our car sped, the number of busses or other vehicles was really less on those uneven roads but the road was packed with black and green auto rickshaws and cycle rickshaws. The number of people on the roads and alleys was much less in comparison to Dhaka, but the markets and shops were stuffed with consumer goods. There was a sense of calmness and pure serenity in Tangail that could only be felt. There was a kind of magnetic attraction in that city that made me feel at home as soon as I entered it; I could feel an attachment.

After some time, the driver told me that we had reached the location of Roshan Ara's phone number. It was a residential complex. Before entering the complex I dialed her number so that I could inform Abdul Manna Sahab about my arrival, but even after several rings nobody answered the phone from the other side. I asked the driver to park the car and requested him to come along with me to the said address. It was an apartment in an old building that had lost all its color and luster, there was nobody at the main entrance meaning anyone and everyone could enter the building undeterred. On the fourth floor, it was a corner flat; the corridor had a cement wall on one side whereas the other side had an iron grill. There was a grill door outside the apartment door, which was locked from the inside. I pressed the doorbell a couple of times but I could feel it, the bell did not make any sound anywhere, neither inside the apartment nor outside. I shook the iron gate gently and it created a faint noise as if startled by my actions. The driver, looking at my elegant ways, smiled gently and said, "Excuse me." When I moved aside, he stood on his toes and, putting his hands inside the iron door, unlatched the lock. And then he banged on the door loudly with the car keys. In no time, a feeble voice of a woman was heard from the inside.

Okhane ke? "Who is there?"

The driver replied loudly, *Amra Abdul Mana ke dekhte chai?* "We want to meet Abdul Manan."

The woman said in the same feeble voice without opening the door, *Manan barite nei.* "Manan is not at home."

Shey kokhon phirey aashbe. "When will he be back?" the driver asked.

Sandhyay. "Evening," was the response.

I asked the driver with a hand gesture about the conversation; he told me everything in one sentence. "He is not at home. He will be back in the evening."

I told him to ask about Roshan Ara to which he cried, Aapni ki janen Roshan Ara? "Do you know Roshan Ara?"

The question made the person on the end become silent for a while.

Amara sathe mariyamera kan'ya phatima'o achena yara pakistana theke ra'osana arara sathe dekha karate esechena.

"I have the daughter of Maryam Fatma with me who has come down from Pakistan to meet Roshan Ara," the driver said, making the most of the silence told her about the motive of my arrival.

The silence persisted on the other end, but then a soft voice said from the inside, Aapni pore aashen. "You come back later."

Kataksana? "How long?" the driver asked.

Sandhyaya. "Evening." Once again the same reply came from the other end.

I looked at the driver hopelessly; he shook his shoulders in dejection and gestured for me to return. Both of us came back and sat in the car thinking, *Do we sit here the whole day and wait for Abdul Manan or return back to Dhaka?*

After some time, I told the driver, "I don't think we should stay here anymore."

The driver agreed with me. "Yeah, it's only an hour's drive; we can come back in the evening."

I told him, "Let's go back to the hotel."

As it is it was just 10:00 in the morning, instead of roaming all around the city and keeping the vehicle busy it was better that we returned to the hotel I thought. The driver sped towards the highway once again; I took a long breath feeling hopeless, and resting my back against the seat I stared at the ceiling silently.

The traffic on our way back from Tangail was a little slow, yet still we made it to the hotel by noon. On my return, I was engulfed by a sense of despair and dejection; I tried to analyze everything from a practical point of view and reached the conclusion that the behavior of Abdul Manan and his wife was not very abnormal. Obviously, they were not duty bound to me or others to accommodate me as and when I wanted. It was I who had made a one-sided plan and come down to Bangladesh, it was not necessary that everything happened as I wished. I was there looking for age-old relationships and who knew how serious those ties were? These thoughts ran through my head at their own pace. Chances were Ammi might have got those pictures from someone and I was uselessly trying to infer some conclusions from them and in this connection making my life difficult listening to Zosia and her family stories.

The more deeply I thought of everything the more frustrated I felt at my own stupidity and not the lack of support I received from Abdul Manan and his wife. *How can I go so deeply into something so meaningless, and not only that, how can I come all the way to Bangladesh from Pakistan just on a whim? But then why did Ammi keep those letters and pictures so carefully in her diary?* My thoughts began to scatter in opposite directions. *Why did that weird-looking man in the graveyard jump on the pictures?* I should have asked Zosia more about Peter and also informed her about the pages of Ammi's diary. After all, he was the same Peter who had come to East Pakistan because both Zosia and Ammi had the same picture. In the letter of Ammi, Zosia had clearly expressed her disapproval of his joining the army and going to East Pakistan. Once again my train of thoughts ran in favor of my decision; no way, I was not there for nothing I consoled myself. I felt confident that I was going to solve the whole mystery. The clouds of hopelessness and despair began to part and then I got a new ray of light. Shuffling around inside my bag I took out the visiting card of Kalpana Dutta, dialed the hotel lobby, gave them Kalpana's number, and asked them to dial her for me. On hearing her hello, I reminded her of our meeting the day before and asked her to schedule a meeting with me. Kalpana recognized me immediately and told me she was going to be in the Liberation War Museum the whole day today. She also told me that if I wanted I could meet her at 2:00 in the afternoon. I googled the directions from the hotel to the museum, it was just 25 minutes away; I dialed the kitchen and ordered them to send lunch to my room and to get rid of the fatigue I went to the washroom to freshen up.

◆

Getting down to the Liberation War Museum, I told my driver that he could leave right away—once I finish my work there, I would call him directly. My new surroundings and zero knowledge of the Bengali language made me trust the ride provided by the hotel more than a local taxi. There was a sense of gloom in the building of the Liberation War Museum, it seemed the cement and bricks of the building were smeared with the tears and grief of the people of Bangladesh. The walls were discolored as if painted with the broken hearts of their people. The environment was dense with silent cries and muffled lamentations. I saw the time; it was 2:00 p.m. There was a woman sitting at the desk, I enquired about Kalpana's office and she directed me towards the interior building of the museum. As I took a step towards her office, I could see her come along with a group of people who looked like foreigners to me. The moment she saw me, she waved out at me enthusiastically and gestured with her hands to go to her. I could see she was giving out details about the museum to the visitors; halting mid-sentence, she introduced me to the people with her and also invited me to take a look at the museum with them. The majority of visitors were Europeans and it was evident from their appearance that they were university students.

We walked through different galleries of the museum and Kalpana filled them with information about each gallery one after another. On the first floor, she narrated the early history of Bangladesh—during the Indian War of Independence the armed and non-armed contributions of the Bengalis to fight the battle against the British Raj—and the students present compared the modern revolution with a couple of other revolutions. On reaching the second floor, we saw the movement of the Bengali language, the revolution of Sheikh Mujib-ur-Rahman, the spilling of blood of the Bangladeshi students in the year 1952 at Dhaka University, and the reaction of West Pakistan, debates and discussions over the national language. I could see Kalpana was discussing all these subjects in great detail in a very friendly and casual manner. The truth is, just like the rest of them, I was captivated by her personality.

When she reached the next gallery of the museum, I saw it exhibited the Guerilla War of Pakistan with Mukti Bahini in 1971, the genocide of millions of innocent Bangladeshis, and the mass rape and humiliation of women; there were images, statues, and weapons that spoke of the horrors of history in total gore. Her words falling on my ears began to change shape, they danced in front of my eyes like smoky shapes and I could hear the cries of women and children. As I passed through the dozens of human skulls and skeletons placed inside the galleries, I felt embarrassed; I felt I was also a part of this oppression and atrocity. I hung my head in silence and stared at my toes and then I thought, *I was born in Bengal, why am I blaming myself?* I felt this was the only fact that was preventing me from holding myself responsible for such horrors, but even then I don't know why I recited this poetry of Faiz Ahmed Faiz inside my head:

We are still strangers, after so many hospitalities
How many meetings will it take to feel connected again?

When will I see the lush of the colorless spring?
How long will it take to wash away the stains of blood?

The final moments of love were excruciating
The mornings were merciless after nights of mercy

My heart wanted but the brokenness didn't give me a chance
Would have listen to complaints after begging for hours

As Faiz went to propose gifting own life in return
Those words remained unsaid after talking about things that didn't
matter at all

———————◆———————

After the visit of the European students, Kalpana took me to her
office. She asked me to take a seat, offering me tea, and she asked
me the reason for the meeting.

"How may I help you?"

I told her everything from the beginning to the end—the migration
of Ammi from Bangladesh to Pakistan, her diary, pictures, Roshan
Ara, Shamshad Begam, and their phones. In fact, I also told her
about Zosia, and Peter too, and then I asked her, "Are you going to
help me solve this mystery?"

"This is a very difficult matter, Fatma," Kalpana replied. "It was a
matter of ninety thousand soldiers and it's been such a long time
too. Who are we going to search for his name on this list? Provided
such a list even exists."

"Hmm," was all I could come up with on hearing her. Finishing my
tea, I rose to leave. "Let me leave then."

"Sorry," and then Kalpana asked me, "Will you go back to the
hotel?"

"Yes." To this Kalpana offered me a ride to the hotel. "I am going
the same way," she said.

On our way back, she continued to talk about me for a long time; maybe she was trying to get a better understanding of my issue. This was perhaps the reason why, when we reached the hotel, she said, "I have another idea; if you agree, we can try it tomorrow."

And at that time I asked myself whether I had any option other than agreeing with her.

CHAPTER 16

The next day, early morning, Asad called up again. I could see that my stay in Bangladesh was making him a tad nervous. After exchanging greetings and casual conversation, he asked how successful I had been in my endeavor. He was of the opinion that this adventure was nothing more than a whim. This was exactly the same idea that caught me in its trap several times, which is why Asad's assumptions did not trouble me much. During the conversation, it slipped from his mouth that he was going to be in Jammu and Kashmir for a couple more days, this information gave me a jolt because at that time Kashmir was surrounded by the Indian army on all sides. I said, "Can I ask you something?"

"Sure, why not? I am using WhatsApp," Asad informed me.

I knew that normally WhatsApp calls are encrypted, which is why it is restricted in the intelligence department or army, and now, since Asad was in Jammu and Kashmir, he was given permission to use WhatsApp alone. Finally, I asked him.

"Are you involved in the insurgencies with the Indian army?"

"Fatma, these are common occurrences herein at the border and beyond the borders as well," Asad replied.

"And what about the innocent Kashmiris who suffer because of all this?" I asked.

"This is what creates news in the international press and India and Pakistan are fighting a media war," Asad informed me. "Listen, this is nothing new; at the LoC (Line of Control), armies from both sides are constantly into such small tiffs. Consider it a kind of silent contract of Inter-Establishment; it's all a part of a power game. If these small ambushes don't take place then both the budget and political influence and impact of the two countries will suffer and slacken. The world is confined in the color, caste, religion, ethnicity, communal and sectarian ghettos and all the differences arise from these walls."

I listened to everything silently. The moment he finished, I said, "What about the genocide of the innocents? The mass gang rape of women, orphaned children, people turning into refugees, what is all this?"

Asad took a deep breath and said, "Fatma, the truth is the world is divided into two classes, the oppressed and the oppressor. The history of the world is divided into these two classes only."

"And you are with them?" This time I asked him blatantly.

Asad, who had been talking continuously till now, became silent.

"Tell me, who are you with? Are you with the oppressed or the oppressor?" I repeated my question. "Are you going to erect more walls in these ghettos or bring down the wall?"

Asad remained silent; maybe he was not expecting such a question from me. "Asad, if you are with the persecuted then you are with me; if you are one of those to bring down the ghetto walls then you are with me; if you are with those who will wipe away tears then you are with me else we are not one, Asad. I will wait for your answer." I disconnected the call.

After some time, I changed into fresh attire and went downstairs to the lounge and dropped a message for Kalpana at the reception desk. Then I went to the cafeteria for breakfast.

———————◆———————

It was a pleasant surprise to see Kalpana busy talking to a group of people in the cafeteria. I felt she was there way before me but being in the queue for the café I could not have noticed her earlier. Looking at me, she waved enthusiastically from a distance and signaled from her hand for me to join her. She told me that she had reached the hotel only a little while ago, and instead of going to my room, she came to the cafeteria looking for me. She told me that she would take out some time from the office and try to meet people working in Central Library Research, Security Intelligence, Dhaka, and also a few people in the office of HRB, a few of whom she knew personally. It felt good to see that Kalpana was taking my life story and my personal investigation seriously, she didn't ignore it, calling it a mere whim, because the previous night, after talking to her, I had got the impression that she was only trying to pacify me.

In no time, our drive was crawling at Kazi Nazrul Islam University because, despite all our efforts, even in the morning all the rickshaws, buses, cars, and trucks crowded the road and trapped us on all sides. The traffic was extremely slow and I could see that on either side of the main road people hurried on the pavements and sped towards their destination to make sure they were on time. I could feel the condition of the people sitting in this lazy traffic was no different, everyone sitting in their respective vehicles was as eager to reach their destination as those who were running on the pavement. There were commercial skyscrapers on both sides, high-rise residential complexes, shops, banks, educational centers, and shopping malls that made me feel as if was in Karachi or Lahore. The same noise and pollution on the road, the same rush outside different office buildings; in fact, people ran on the pavements in exactly the same manner there as they did back home, they carried the same anxiety and stress on their faces; there was nothing, nothing that made me feel I was not in Pakistan at that time. Suddenly, the voice of Kalpana brought me back to the world inside the car from the hullabaloo of the city life outside and I was back in Bangladesh from Pakistan.

"How did you feel about Bangladesh in these two or three days?" Before I could reply, she tried to rephrase her sentence. "I know it's a very short time to develop an opinion, but still...."

"I just realized from your question that I am in Dhaka instead of Lahore or Karachi." I voiced my thoughts.

"Yeah, you're right, other than the language we aren't so different. Our cultures, customs, values, and religion are the same." She pressed hard on the horn as a truck tried to overtake her car and said, "You are right, the same corruption, political and military issues, religious extremism, and the same illiteracy and poverty.

"Yeah, these things are still going on in our society. But we've learned a lot from Pakistan's history, especially from the Liberation War of 1971, and we are seriously solving these issues.

"We are improving every day. If you were to look at the social and economic indexes and compare them with Pakistan, you would see what I mean," she continued, swerving the car to Ruqaiya Begam Colony.

"But I don't know if Pakistan's learned any lesson from '71's Liberation War and the partition of Pakistan."

I remained silent because maybe I knew the answer way too well, maybe at that time I avoided being a freak, but it's a fact that I had always had doubts regarding Pakistan's internal and foreign political policies because I knew these were the two basic nails in the coffin of Pakistan's economy, and for the past 74 years they had continued to hammer them in all the wrong places.

In order to avoid political discussion, I said, "Yeah, you may be right. Can I ask you something personal?"

"Yeah, why not? But I know what you are going to ask because we girls can be from anywhere but we still think the same thing." She grinned. "You're going to ask whether I'm married or not and how many kids I have, right?" A smile spread across my lips.

"Yeah, I'm married and I have two kids. My husband, Arun Datta, is attached to Dhaka Security Intelligence. I spoke to him about you last night and he said that it's a matter of some time, but he'd look into it on his own. To be honest, Fatma, he's not very hopeful that he'll find anything, but he'll put Peter Casnova's name into the system and will see if it's entrapped anywhere so we can get his background."

"You're already doing a lot for me." I was genuinely grateful for all her efforts.

"No need to thank me, I'm happy I could help you," Kalpana replied, swiping her card at the entrance to the Liberation War Museum parking lot and seeing the gates open.

On reaching the office, she looked at her day's assignments and called up her secretary, she told her to book an appointment with the Central Library Dhaka Research Cell and Human Rights office of Bangladesh. While I was busy browsing different magazines in her office, she was busy finishing her work. During that time she also told me that for a few hours she would be going to Dhaka University to give a presentation, Central Library was a very short distance away. Kalpana's secretary called and said she had booked an appointment at noon in Central Library and at 3:30 with the director of the Human Rights office. In the next two hours, Kalpana completed all her work and I took another round of the Liberation War Museum; she then took me to Dhaka University, which was only twenty minutes from her office.

While walking down the university corridor, I thought no matter how old or dilapidated is the building of an educational institute the plants there look so different and no matter how different the students may appear, act, or sound they carry the same intellectual exuberance all around the world.

Kalpana's presentation was in the auditorium of the Political Science department where she was to give a speech on the psychological condition of the orphans and foster children during the 1971 war. I took the back row so that the students could sit in the front. Soon after the introduction, the lights were turned off and the screen broadcasted a 30-minute BBC documentary on the Bangladesh genocide followed by which Kalpana showed pictures of orphaned and adopted children who were born in different hospitals, lived in shelter homes, and raised in orphanages. During the third phase of the presentation, she narrated their mental illnesses; my mind wandered off to Zosia's story and I began to think that it was possible that, during childhood, Zosia, Johan, Selena, Jacob and Aidan looked different than these Bengali kids physically but their psychological states were exactly the same—shattered and torn.

Coming down from the stage, Kalpana tapped on her wristwatch indicating that we must leave the university instantly because only a few minutes were left until noon. After walking swiftly for some time, we were sitting face-to-face with an aged gentleman from the Central Research Library Cell. Kalpana told me on our way that Dr. Mahmood ul Hasan was not just a librarian but was also a retired professor of history and the author of a couple of books. Working as a librarian at the university was just a hobby. After listening to my entire story from Kalpana, he touched his bald head and then, looking at me, he told her something in Bengali. I did not ask Kalpana to translate it for me because the way he said it, his expression, and his gestures explained everything to me that my suspicions on the basis of pictures and letters were completely baseless and a waste of time. He was under the impression that Kalpana wanted to meet him to gain some information on important historical events and my frustrated self took him as some mediocre retired professor who shunned my curiosity without even listening to everything attentively.

"Do you think the same way?" I asked Kalpana on our way back.

"Not at all, Fatma. If that was the case why would I have talked to a history professor or the Office of Human Rights for you?"

"Okay, tell me something, Kalpana." Looking at the traffic from the car, I asked her, "If you'd found some letters and photos of your mother after her death, as I have, wouldn't you also have tried to find out more about their background?"

"Yeah, I would've done the same thing, but don't forget that this is also a part of our age. In our youth, we are always involved in some sort of excitement and we lived in the hope of something new happening every evening. But as we start to grow up, we start to lose this misconception." In that one sentence Kalpana tried to protect the prestige of the professor and console my heart in such a manner that she could bridge the gap between my assumptions and practicalities.

On reaching the Liberation War Museum, once again Kalpana got busy with her work and began to look at the books and magazines in her office, and soon it was 4:00 p.m. and both of us left for HRB. On our way, we bought sandwiches from McDonald's. My experience at the Human Rights office was twice as depressing and futile when they offered me a long tedious form after hearing my story, attached a photocopy of my passport and identity card with that form and filed everything and then told me everything in their own type of English.

"We will let you know the outcome of our complaint investigation into you." I could only smile in response to this.

The ride back to the hotel was silent, with blank eyes I grasped the noise of the city and the silence within, which was why, when Kalpana said something, without paying much attention to it I gave her monosyllabic replies. As she was able to understand what was going through my head, she did not find it reasonable to proceed further, but when we reached the hotel gates, she told me that in the office Arun had called and despite going through the computer screen several times, he could not find any entry under the name of

149

Peter Casnova. This did not surprise me much because by now I was of the firm belief that this trip to Bangladesh was just a waste of time and money. On getting down from the car, once again I thanked her for all her help and support; she stared at me for a little longer than normal and then said, "Be ready in the morning, we'll both go to Tangail to meet Abdul Mannan."

"But Manaan sahib didn't even try to contact the hotel after we left a few messages for him. Maybe his contacts are also meaningless, like Roshan Ara, Shamshad Begam, Peter, Zosia's photos, and the pages of her diary," I replied dejectedly.

"No, I'll call Manaan sahib from Arun's office tomorrow and I'm sure he won't be late in contacting us after that. Whatever happens, be ready tomorrow. I'll take half a day off from work tomorrow to get this done."

I felt only a woman can understand a woman's pain and I agreed despairingly.

On reaching the hotel, I was once again flooded by thoughts of Asad. I turned on the laptop and checked my inbox, but there was no email. I don't know why, but I emailed him this couplet by Parveen Shakir.

No courage to move, impossible to stay

This journey of love has left me lifeless

But then, on second thoughts, I deleted it and turned off the laptop. I lay down on the bed and stared at the ceiling silently and then closed my eyes.

CHAPTER 17

Two hours went by swiftly but there was no sign of Kalpana. I tried calling her a couple of times but her phone remained constantly busy. At noon I began to feel restless, I was left with just one day in Dhaka because it was Thursday and my flight was booked for the Saturday. The truth is after the previous day's frustration, this restlessness was quite surprising for me, but I felt Abdul Mannan alone was my last hope in Dhaka. If I got to know anything about Roshan Ara from him then surely I would go meet her tomorrow, and if this didn't happen then I would request Kalpana to reach Roshan Ara and remain in touch with her from Karachi. During the morning I went to the lounge a number of times, asked the receptionist, and peeked at the cafeteria now and then; in fact, I also went to the gate waiting to see her car, but she was nowhere to be found. Soon, it was 04:00 and I felt utterly dejected. I thought after the previous day's episode I had wasted my time trusting Kalpana. I wished I had gone to Tangail on my own with the driver, who knows I might have got a chance to meet with Abdul Manan. Suddenly, I thought, *Why don't I leave for Tangail now? He is home in the evening only, that's what the lady said.* I went to the reception and asked for a ride; they informed me that the ride needed to be booked a day earlier. If I wanted, she could book a ride for the next day. I thought, *There is still some time left, I can do this* *in the evening itself, in the meanwhile, I will wait for her a little longer.*

Making my decision, I returned to the room and, lying on the bed, I began to surf through different TV channels. When I got a little bored, I closed my eyes and then I don't know when exactly I fell asleep. On waking up I realized someone was at the door; initially, I thought it was room service and there to clean the room, just checking to see whether someone was in the room or not, but then I thought of Kalpana. Getting up instantly, I went to the door and looked outside through the spyhole. I was right, it was Kalpana standing outside, and there was also a man in his 50s with her. He looked like a typical Bengali. When I opened the door, she smiled at me and asked, "May we come in?"

I moved back instantly and said, "Please come in."

Kalpana introduced me to the man with her. "This is Abdul Manan."

I saw he was a man of medium height, thin with a brownish complexion clad in a gray-colored striped shirt with a pocket. He was wearing thick glasses; his thick hair and mustache were peppered with signs of aging. He stared at me closely and then stood against the wall like a convict. After a while, Kalpana looked at me and said, "I know you've been waiting for me all day."

"No, it's okay, I understand you must be busy." I smiled and tried to conceal my day's restlessness.

"But I was busy with your things. I was trying to contact National Security Intelligence and Mr. Manan—" She gestured towards Manan Sahab but I interrupted her mid-sentence.

"Both of you please feel comfortable. Come, sit here on the sofa and then we can talk peacefully." I addressed the two of them and waved towards the couch. Manan Sahab put up his right hand in the air and tried to say that he was okay standing by the wall. Kalpana sat on the sofa and I took a seat opposite her on the edge of my bed.

"Mr. Manan has just come from Tangail at my request. I informed him that you are Maryam's daughter and wanted to get some information about Roshan Ara, whom she was in contact with before her death. Mr. Manan just told me that Maryam was his ex-wife who left Pakistan with her two-to-three-year-old daughter after her divorce. Roshan Ara was Maryam's mother, who died in 1998."

Kalpana continued to drone in her usual tone and each of her words to my ears was like an explosive. In the explosion, one thing repeated over and over again: "Maryam was his ex-wife," and this sentence ricocheted through my brain like a bullet. I turned towards Manan Sahab and I could see that, despite the fact he didn't understand a word of English, he knew way too well what Kalpana was talking about. Averting his gaze from me, he stared at the floor and I wanted to take a clear look at his face to know what exactly was there—guilt, regret, happiness, pain, grief, hatred, or long-lost love? I wanted to look into his eyes to see if there was any sign of me in those eyes or not. But all I saw there was a man silently standing in the corner with his head bent down staring at the floor. And I was thinking, *Is he my father?* His language, features, and eyes, nothing resembled me, he was just some average stranger walking on the road to whom I had asked my address and he had replied that he did not belong to my locality. I looked at Manan Sahab for some time and when I could take it no more, I excused myself and ran towards the washroom. Closing the door I burst into bitter sobs.

After some time I heard Kalpana knocking on the bathroom door. I splashed water on my face and dabbed it against a towel, but the red circles around my eyes gave away the condition of my heart. When I came out, Manan Sahab was not there; maybe he had lost all courage to face me. It was good for him that I didn't know how to speak Bengali as he didn't have any language to converse with me in. Kalpana held me gently by both shoulders and made me sit on the sofa. Before talking, she handed me a glass of water and gestured for me to drink. With my head bent down, I took small sips of water silently and Kalpana continued to pat my shoulder and back affectionately. She then told me, "I can comprehend the pain you are going through on hearing this, but I need you to have more courage for what I'm about to tell you. This may be more painful than what you've just experienced." I gave her a blank look and placed the glass on the table.

"I was informed by Manan that Roshan Ara was one of the million girls and women who were victimized in Bengal during the genocide of 1971. Roshan Ara was only 14 years old when she was kidnapped, raped, and held in an army camp for months. She was also pregnant like other girls when she was found after Operation Searchlight. Your mother Maryam was like the others whose fathers were not known. She had suspicions about a man named Peter Casnova since her features were more Western. Roshan Ara later moved with Maryam to Tangail as her parents and other relatives rejected her. Maryam grew up in Tangail where she was married to Manan, but the marriage fell apart within two or three years since Manan didn't tolerate her as he felt she was a bastard girl. Frustrated and angry, Maryam left Bangladesh and moved to Pakistan with Roshan Ara's diary and photos of Peter."

I knew Kalpana was speaking the truth because Manan Sahab's absence proved the authenticity of every word.

"Do you want to see Mr. Manan one last time?" Kalpana asked me one last time before she left as she knew he was sitting downstairs in the lounge.

"No." And that's when I locked my door from inside.

The next day, I remained locked inside my room.

My mind felt numb; there were no thoughts except for a sense of drowsiness due to immense tiredness. I kept thinking about Kalpana; the lanes of Dhaka, the roads, Shahid Minar, Parliament House, the fort, the library and university kept rotating around my head, I also wandered off to the Liberation War Museum for some time but then returned pretty quickly. For a while I roamed through the alleys of Tangail, the market, shops and moss-covered buildings, but in the midst of all this, not even for a second did I think of Abdul Manan.

Yes, finally, when my flight left from Dhaka Airport to Karachi, I was once again engulfed by Tagore and that was the last time I looked at Roshan Ara and Maryam's Dhaka, and with tearful eyes and a choked voice, I hummed Tagore's poem under my breath.

O Lord
In my arid heart

Rain is halted
Since so many days
And the sky
Is bare to the point of inhumanity
The signs of soft cloud
Not even a thin thread is seen
From somewhere cool sprinkles
Are not to be seen

If this is your wish
Draped in the darkness of death
Send in your storm of wrath
Lashes of lightning
From the seventh heaven
One horizon to the next
Drench me in purity

But o my Master
That thing seeping inside my heart
A fire of silence
Take it back
One that's still, sharp and fast
With hopelessness in the heart
Making it feel despair
The day Father's wrath will come down
Just like the sad face of a mother
You wrap in your cloak of mercy

CHAPTER 18

O n reaching home I realized I didn't return empty-handed, I was carrying those lost pages of history that I was trying to find in Zosia's diary that changed its geographical location; with the wind of East Europe it flew off to Bangladesh and from there reached Kashmir. The color of those words was still as red as it was hundreds of years ago. Nothing had changed, neither the sword-like sharpness of the pen nor the soft baby-like texture of papers; even now the diaries were filled with the silent sobs of the tortured and oppressed, and even now the pages were inscribed with shivering hands.

In the evening, I called Zosia a couple of times but one particular message kept repeating itself: "The number you have called is currently switched off. Please try to call after some time." I thought maybe her phone had gone bad and I should go visit her the next day. The following day was Sunday and I could wait one more day to relieve the stress of the Bangladesh trip. A corner of my heart kept waiting for Asad, there was no email or call from his side in the last two days. On turning on the laptop I saw there was no email from his side, I thought I must write him something, but then I thought of the things I had told him earlier, this stopped me from trying anything. When I called Atya, she was home and said, "You must be tired; come, have dinner with us in the evening," but I refused. Firstly, I didn't have any strength in me to drive at that time and, secondly, I knew she would ask me about the Bangladesh trip. I had no wish to narrate those stories to her. On disconnecting the call, I called up McDonald's, placed my order, and then, lying in bed, I watched TV.

I woke up early the next morning. After finishing breakfast, I took my car and went to Zosia's house. I was taken aback by the sight of a huge lock hanging outside her house. It looked as though nobody had been home for a week or two and I could feel a thick layer of depression around the house. Feeling restless, I rang the bell of her neighbor, Tahseen Jaffry. I waited for some time but there was no response, I thought it was maybe due to it being Sunday, they were having a lie-in. I returned to my car and sat inside; I thought, *Why not go to Atya's instead of home?* When I called her, she was eager to meet me as usual.

On seeing me at the door she said, "I have been waiting for your return for the past week."

"Is everything okay?" I asked.

"My pregnancy test is positive." She was jumping with joy. I hugged her happily, for the past two years she had been going crazy to conceive. From the very beginning, she was simply crazy about kids and always dreamed of having a huge family. She told me, "It's good you are here, we'll go shopping in a while."

I thought, *Why not? It will help me de-stress my tired nerves.*

In the afternoon, when our car passed through the Shahid Millat Road, looking at the traffic and the buildings on either side of the road I was suddenly teleported to the Qazi Nazrul Islam Avenue of Dhaka; at that time, I found myself in Bangladesh instead of

Karachi. But soon enough, just like Kalpana had done, Atya too pulled me back to reality with her question. "Well, won't you tell me how you found Dhaka?"

I looked at her in the same manner as I had looked at Kalpana and smiled. "Bro, this Dhaka and Karachi are one and the same, they only have different names."

"I too feel the same," Atya agreed with me. "They were a part of the same nation, how can they be different then? Same old history, geography, culture, and corrupt politicians...."

This made me laugh; I always found a melodious tone in Atya's speech.

"And what about your mission?" she asked after remaining silent for some time.

"More or less done, all you can say is that I just need to meet with Zosia now so that I can understand everything completely." I gave her an honest reply.

But I was sure she didn't understand a thing. Maybe I too wanted the same.

The remainder of the day was spent at Dalmon shopping. I could see how excitedly Atya was looking at the baby dresses. Within a few days, her face had become flushed with the affectionate colors of pregnancy.

———————◆———————

When I reached home that night, a voicemail from Rauf Sahab awaited me. He was as excited as Atya; he was saying that his TV channel had finally been approved by PEMRA, something he had been working on for the past six months. So far it was good news, but the latter part was not very convenient for me because he informed me that the next day, for an urgent meeting, I was to leave for Islamabad where I was to meet a few members of PBA and clear their doubts about certain fields so that this final stage could be accomplished. He was busy with an important meeting in Karachi; hence, except for me, he didn't have anyone capable enough for this job.

I breathed a sigh and slumped on the bed. Then, suddenly, a new idea cropped up in my head that made new energy surge inside my body. I remembered that during my university days, Asad always spoke about joining the media. This thought made me call up Rauf Sahab instantly and confirm my decision to go to Islamabad.

◆

The next few days went by attending meetings in Islamabad. During each of the meetings, I impressed the members of the Pakistan Broadcast Association with my impeccable speech and with my convincing power did my best to expiate all their doubts regarding the channel. Whenever I got a chance, I tried to reach Zosia over the phone, but it did not give me anything new except for the same old recorded message. On reaching Karachi, I saw Rauf Sahab at the airport who had come to greet me. The constant smile on his face said everything. He was extremely happy with my progress and wanted to discuss some new plans about the channel with me, but despite all things positive and happy, I felt my heart sinking. Initially, I thought it was all because of stuff that happened in

Dhaka, I blamed it on the disturbing things I came to know about Roshan Ara and Ammi, but now I was feeling anxious about Asad too because, in the meantime, there had been no contact from his end. In his last call, he had told me that he was posted to Jammu and Kashmir, a place surrounded by the Indian army on all sides. On my return journey from Islamabad, I had made up my mind that if he didn't contact me that day either, I would push aside my ego and call him on WhatsApp from my end.

On reaching home, I erased the last drop of ego from my heart and checked my email nervously. I saw a heartwarming poem by Parveen Shakir waiting for me in my inbox sent by Asad.

On the path of helplessness
What a strange intersection
On one side there is no horizon
Darkness without light
Isolation without cloak
Unlimited humiliation
Selfless sacrifice
Silent loneliness without a sound
Degradation without bounds
Heart-wrenching grief
And on the other side
Confined in love
Violation of heart

Yours
Asad

The next day, on returning from the office, I once again went to Zosia's house and once again I faced the same depression and the same old huge lock outside her door. It was 5:00 in the evening, I thought maybe Tahseen must be home now, so I rang the bell. After two minutes a young man opened the door and, hearing the name of Tahseen Sahab from me, went back inside. After some time, Tahseen Sahab came to the door rubbing his eyes, I thought the poor thing must have been taking a nap. He was taken aback to see me there; then something made him invite me inside his home. Asking me to sit in the living room, he went inside and changed into something presentable; he was also looking a lot fresher now.

When I asked him about Zosia, he looked very surprised and said, "Hey! Don't you know? Zosia passed away a few weeks ago."

I was stunned by the information and my heart sank further.

"But I spoke with her only a few days ago over the phone," I blurted.

"A few days, what do you mean?" He was surprised.

"I mean two to three weeks back." I rectified my statement.

I recalled that two days before leaving for Bangladesh I had called Zosia and at that time she sounded very weak, when I expressed my wish to meet her, she had excused herself very politely.

"Last week I was in Bangladesh and a week prior to that and even after returning back I was fairly occupied in my office, meaning it's been almost three weeks since I last spoke with her," I stated very softly.

"Yes, of course, it has been three weeks since this tragedy. She had a cardiac arrest; I took her to the hospital but she passed away within two days," he informed me.

"Oh, God!" I blurted involuntarily and then I continued to stare at the floor.

The two of us remained silent for a while. Zosia's face flashed through my eyes continuously, I could not believe that she was no more. After some time, I tried to take my leave from Tahseen Sahab and got up to go. No sooner did I reach the main door than something came to his mind and Tahseen Sahab asked me to wait for two minutes and went inside. When he returned, I could see he was carrying Zosia's diary in his hand. Giving me the diary he said, "In the hospital, Zosia told me that if something happened to her I was to hand the diary to you."

I saw her diary was stuffed with pictures and dog-eared pages, the only difference was that Tahseen Sahab had tied an elastic band around it so that nothing could escape from the pages. Taking the diary from him I asked, "Do you know where she is buried?"

"Certainly! I was present during her final rites. The Gora Kabristan (white cemetery) next to National Stadium, she is buried there," he told me.

"Can we go there? Either today or tomorrow?" I asked him nervously because I was not close enough to him that I could ask him for a favor so blatantly; moreover, I knew how dangerous it was for a lone girl to go to a graveyard.

"Sure. If you want, the two of us can go there right now because I will be out of town during the weekend and, post that, I will be busy with office work." He asked me to wait for a while. He once again

163

went inside. Most probably he went inside to tell his wife that he was going to the cemetery with me. On his return, he was carrying his car keys.

On our way to the graveyard, I saw a flower shop, I requested him to stop there for a while.

As soon as the car entered the cemetery, I began to look around subconsciously. I thought the man who only a few months ago tried to enter my vehicle by force could be somewhere around, but then I understood I was just being paranoid. He was not there.

After parking the car, we passed through the muddy path between the graves and reached a spot of fresh graves. Zosia's grave had her name written with charcoal on a wooden slab; seeing it Tahseen Sahab stopped and said, "It's here. I have ordered an epitaph, it will be ready soon."

On seeing the grave, my heart bled as tears welled up in my eyes and then one after another I remembered all our meetings. I remembered how she always welcomed me into her home and spoke ever so affectionately and lovingly. I remembered the elegance with which she prepared tea and coffee for me. I remembered how she confided in me her life story and grief. I remained silent and stared at her grave. I thought, *I wish I hadn't gone to Bangladesh last week; I wish I'd stayed here two weeks back and tended to her in her last days; I wish I'd held her hand in the hospital during her final moments. ...I wish, I wish, I wish!*

Had Zosia been alive I would have informed her that I had found a few missing pages of her life in the warmth of Bangladesh and the arms of the Kashmir Valley, and just like hers, I found these pages stained with the blood of Kashmiri and Bangladeshi women. With my head bent, I stared at the grave standing forlorn. The clouds of memories engulfed me from all sides and my grief streamed through my eyes in thick droplets of tears. Soon, Tahseen Sahab covered the grave with the wreath I'd bought and, raising his hands, he offered prayers. I also raised my hands in prayer.

As we were leaving, Tahseen Sahab pointed toward another fresh grave and said that that grave belonged to her son. I whispered, "Peter," and he nodded in agreement. For a minute I thought I should go to his grave, but then I thought of Ammi and Roshan Ara, and in that very instant I turned away my face. I told Tahseen Sahab that my mother was buried nearby and I wanted to go there too.

"Why not? Sure," Tahseen Sahab said, but I felt that this information was a little shocking for him because this cemetery was mainly for Christians. Assuming me to be a new Muslim maybe, he ignored it and walked ahead.

On our return, my head reeled with shock when Tahseen Sahab informed me that Zosia had suffered a heart attack the moment she heard of her son Peter's death.

"Does it mean Peter was outside Pakistan? Because I never saw him home, nor did I ever hear Zosia mention his name," I stated.

"Oh! Didn't she tell you about him?" Slowing down at the signal, Tahseen Sahab said, "Some forty or forty-five years ago, Zosia disowned Peter for unknown reasons. He used to roam about here in this Gora Kabristan; I believe he was a junkie, but even after disowning him, Zosia more or less every day sent him food, but then his mental condition deteriorated so much that Zosia got fed up and stopped visiting him, or maybe she had become too old and also stopped driving."

Tahseen Sahab's words fell on my ears like molten lava; they created the same havoc within me that was done by Kalpana's words just two days ago. I asked him, "Do you have any picture of Peter?"

"No, I don't have any, but most probably you will find some in Zosia's diary." Without averting his eyes from the road he pointed towards the diary with his head.

Removing the elastic band from the diary, when I opened it, I found a few pictures there; one of them was of a young army officer and when I looked at him closely, I realized who it was.

He was the same madman who attacked me in the cemetery—Peter Casnova.

On reaching home, I flicked open the diary agitatedly and began to look at the folded papers one after another. Using the Polish-English translator on Google, I realized that most of the things written there were already narrated to me by Zosia except for this one.

23 marca 1972

Piotr

Straciles prawo do bycia moim synem po tym, cozrobiles w Bangladeszu. Zaluje, ze nie wiesz, cozrobiles, nie cudzolozyles z tymi niewinnymi bengalskimi dziewczynami w Bangladeszu, ale popelniles cudzolóstwo z moja matka i swoja matka. Przepisales strony historii, których zaginionych stron nie chcialem znalezc.

Moje serce i drzwi mojego domu sa na zawsze zamkniete dla Ciebie.

Zosia

23rd March 1972

Peter,

After what you did in Bangladesh you have no right to call me your son. I wish knew what you have done. In Bangladesh, you did not have sex with those innocent Bengali girls but you have had sex with your own mother. You rewrote exactly the same pages of history that were lost in time for me and I did not want to find those missing pages. The door to my heart and home are closed forever for you.

Zosia

I was still lost in the agony of the letter. Suddenly it seemed someone knocked on my door. Wiping away my tears with the back and palm of my hand, I folded the page, put it back in the diary, and placed it inside the drawer. Peeping through the spy hole there was no end to my surprise and happiness—Asad was standing at the door. When I opened it, he kept his backpack to one side and took both my hands in his and we sat on the bed. For a long time he stared at me silently and then, without uttering a word, he took me in his arms.

www.ingramcontent.com/pod-product-compliance
Lightning Source LLC
Chambersburg PA
CBHW071359120626
46546CB00002B/746